Lieutenant-Commander EP Tomkinson, DSO*, RN

HMS URGE

EP TOMKINSON AND
HIS WWII SUBMARINE COMMAND

FRANCIS DICKINSON

Hesketh House

First published 2022

Published in the United Kingdom by Hesketh House Publishing
publishing@heskeths.org.uk

A catalogue for this book is available from the British Library
ISBN 978-1-7397625-1-3

HMS URGE

DAVID ALLEN
HAROLD ASHFORD
WILLIAM ASHFORD
ROBERT ATTEWELL
LESLIE BAXTER
HENRY BOTTING
CYRIL BROWN
ALBERT BRYANT
SIDNEY CHAMBERLAIN
ROBERT DAVISON
FREDERICK DAY
RONALD GOSS
BERNARD GRAY
LAURENCE GROVES
STANLEY HARMAN
REGINALD HELLYER
CHARLEY JACKMAN
WILFRED LAMB
ERIC LAW
RONALD LEEKE
BRIAN LLOYD
JOHN MAIDMENT
FRED MCDIARMID

JOSEPH MCMILLAN
FREDERICK MORRIS
JESSE NORRIS
JOHN O'NEILL
HERBERT OSBORN
JOHN PARKINSON
MALCOLM POOLE
JOHN RANSOME
ROY ROGERS
JOHN ROWLEY
RONALD RUTTER
MARCUS STANGER
EDWARD TOMKINSON
CHARLES TOMS
HENRY TWIST
ERIC VARLEY
HENRY WATTS
WILLIAM WHITE
RICHARD WILDMAN
SAMUEL WILKES
PETER WISEMAN
JOHN WOOLRICH

HMS Urge ship's badge, presented to Bridgend by the Admiralty

CONTENTS

PREFACE

This short book aims to provide an introduction to the story of the life and loss of HMS Urge, the commanding officer EP Tomkinson and the ship's company. It is intended to contribute to the 2022 commemorations of the 80th anniversary of the submarine's last voyage.

In due course the full story of the experiences, achievements and impact of Urge's crew members, naval passengers and civilian passenger who gave their lives on active service on 27 April, 1942 (and one officer who did so the previous year) will be told. There is much we will never know, and few photographs of Urge survive, but with access to official records of both sides, accounts by those who were there and contemporary letters a good picture can be seen. Added to this, the story of the successful search for the wreck of this special submarine spans years of fascinating historical research and maritime archeology.

My grandparents Edward and Myrtle Tomkinson were married on 9 April, 1940. After my grandmother's death in 2007, my family viewed a trunk of her wartime correspondence. This newly viewed material made clear that not only were Urge's ship's company greatly respected within the Submarine Service, but they also had a very high regard for each other. It was equally clear that whatever high standards and wartime successes were achieved under Edward Tomkinson's command, the one thing he and all who served with him wanted most was to win peace and to return home.

I would like to thank all those who have worked to ensure remembrance of Urge and her exceptional ship's company. The full list includes veterans, researchers, historians, maritime archeologists, the Royal Navy, other armed forces, heritage professionals, the people of Bridgend which was affiliated with Urge, journalists, civil servants, members of the Royal Family and many friends. Very special appreciation is due to the University, authorities, armed forces and people of Malta. Most of all I would like to thank the families of those who were lost in Urge for their support, and in particular my parents Bridget and Peter, my brother Jasper and nephew Edward.

Francis Dickinson
April, 2022

FOREWORD

By Vice Admiral Sir Ian McGeoch

In September, 1941 Admiral Weichold, the German Navy's representative in Rome, reported that 'the most dangerous Allied weapon is the submarine'. Of the Allied submarines one of the most dangerous on the Axis supply route to its forces in North Africa was HMS Urge, commanded by Lieutenant-Commander EP ('Tommo') Tomkinson, DSO*, RN. Having already sunk or damaged several Axis supply ships, he carried out a brilliant attack on Italy's most modern battleships, the Vittorio Veneto and the Littorio, as they emerged from the southern end of the Straits of Messina, escorted by four destroyers and zigzagging at high speed. Firing his full salvo of four torpedoes from a range of 3000 yards, Tommo hit the Vittorio Veneto under her aft turret. Although the battleship got back to harbour she was out of action for three critical months, and in April, 1942 Tommo struck again at the Italian fleet, sinking the cruiser Bande Nere in yet another most skilful attack.

Had Tommo survived the War it is unlikely that he would have written a book about his exploits – he was too modest a person to do that. But I think that in recognition of the indispensable part played his officers and men in HMS Urge, all of whom were so tragically lost with him when their submarine struck a mine near Malta at the end of April, 1942, and in memory of all of them, this factual record of one small submarine's outstanding contribution to the defeat of the Axis powers of 1939-45 would be acceptable to him.

It is a reasonable supposition that those who serve in submarines in war are blessed with courage, but not all have the capacity, the determination, the particular skill and, one may say, luck, to wreak great damage on the enemy. Tommo was one of the very best of our submarine captains, not only in achievement, but also as an individual of exceptional character and engaging personality, whose untimely loss the country, and in particular the Royal Navy, could ill afford. 'There and then our best men were killed' (The Odyssey of Homer).

Vice Admiral Sir Ian McGeoch, KCB, DSO, DSC, RN
Ixworth, Suffolk, 2005

Note: Admiral McGeoch's foreword was written in anticipation of this booklet; he died in 2007, but had given permission for its later use.

INTRODUCTION

The Lazaretto, Manoel Island (left), from which Urge sailed on her last voyage

HMS Urge was a British submarine of the Royal Navy (RN) commanded by Lieutenant-Commander Edward Philip Tomkinson, DSO and Bar, RN during World War Two. As part of the 10th Submarine Flotilla based at Manoel Island in Malta, the submarine had an outstanding record of success at a critical time for the island and Allied forces between 1941-42. Urge sank and damaged Axis warships and supply ships, landed and recovered British special forces and Allied secret agents on enemy coasts, and took part in operations to defend Malta convoys.

The island of Malta had a central role in the Second World War from 1940 to 1943, with 1942 marking the height of the siege and bombing campaign against it. Malta's position in the central Mediterranean gave it a strategic importance both for the British and Allied Forces, and for their German and Italian opponents. Maritime supply lines were critical to the outcome of the War for both sides. The heroism of the armed forces and people of Malta have rightly become famous, the island becoming the most bombed place in history.

The experiences, successes, challenges and fate of the courageous people who sailed and fought in Urge will always be part of the naval and military history of World War II. Like many RN vessels, the submarine had a profound alliance with Malta. Today, the wreck also forms part of the island's heritage. Urge's successes played a frontline part in winning a victory against regimes led by Hitler and Mussolini, and the results of the ultimate sacrifice paid by those who lost their lives continue to benefit countless people across the world today. Importantly, these exceptional successes were achieved at a time when the enemy's strength was at its greatest, and the perils and strains facing Britain and the besieged island of Malta were at their height.

Beyond the war account, and an appreciation of the results of the professional skill and gallantry of Urge's ship's company, lies the story of the people themselves. One sailor who joined Urge in 1941 and went on to other things, and therefore survived, later said 'I realised what a good boat I had joined from the captain downward. All the Senior Rates were first class…' (former Leading Stoker Bill Haines). Those who served in Urge were mostly young and all were among the most lively and able in the RN. Submarines offered exciting opportunities, with individual responsibility, potential for progression and camaraderie. In wartime they also made exceptional demands, and required enormous bravery as well as technical and physical capabilities. The right character was essential, given the need to combine a positive and decisive approach with determination, patience and the ability to get on with others in a confined space for long periods. Danger and pressure would appear at a moment's notice to interrupt the exacting routines of life aboard. Losses among even the best were gravely heavy, prompting Winston Churchill to say:

"Of all the branches of men in the forces there is none which shows more devotion and faces grimmer perils than the submariners."

Shortly before dawn on 27 April, 1942, Urge sailed from Malta for Alexandria. A sustained and intense bombing campaign by enemy aircraft had left many of the 10th Flotilla's submarines sunk and damaged, and a decision was taken temporarily to evacuate the submariners' base. Urge's 32 crew members, 11 naval passengers and one civilian passenger were never heard from again. The official view at the time was that an enemy mine struck shortly after leaving Malta was the most probable cause of the loss, but until the wreck was discovered this could not be confirmed.

HRH Prince Philip The Duke of Edinburgh took an interest in and supported the aims of work undertaken on Urge's history from 2016 until his death in 2021. The story had particular resonance for him as his own distinguished World War II RN service had involved facing the same opponents as Lieutenant-Commander Tomkinson and Urge. The story also connected with his and Her Majesty The Queen's famous affiliations with and affection for the island of Malta.

In 2019 a search which took place as part of an international maritime archeology project discovered HMS Urge's wreck, confirming that an enemy mine was the cause of the submarine's loss. The wreck is protected under the laws of Malta and the United Kingdom.

1

HMS URGE'S CONSTRUCTION AND EARLY MONTHS

At the beginning of World War II in 1939 U class submarines were smaller than other British submarines. They had originally been designed to assist RN surface forces with anti-submarine exercises, but due to their small size were found to be particularly effective in the shallow waters of the Mediterranean. They were also mostly of modern design. Against these benefits, the U class were slow, under-armed compared to larger submarines, and could be difficult to handle at sea. Lieutenant Tomkinson had a particular expertise in U class submarines, having been the first lieutenant of the first of the class, HMS Undine, from 1937. CET Warren was one of his leading stokers and they worked together on new diving and surfacing routines and equipment. As this class of submarine was constructed and launched in Barrow-

HMS Undine, the first of the Royal Navy's U class submarines; the bulbous bow was modified for Urge which came later

in-Furness by Vickers-Armstrongs Limited many engineering and other challenges needed solving for the first time. Warren would later gain fame as the author of Above Us the Waves and other books as well as his film work relating to his submarine experiences. Three years later, after passing his Commanding Officer's Qualifying Course (known as the 'Perisher') and a short period of command of the older submarine HMS H33, Lieutenant Tomkinson took charge of Urge in September, 1940 as she was being built by Vickers-Armstrongs Limited in the same Barrow shipyard that Undine had been.

Chief Engine Room Artificer (CERA) Charles Toms, Leading Seaman Jesse Norris and Leading Signalman Eric Law were among those who joined at this early stage.

Undine seen from the air returning from a deep dive

Together with these early crew members, Lieutenant Tomkinson oversaw fitting out, and he accepted the submarine on behalf of the RN at commissioning on 12 December, 1940. By 20 December, Urge had completed the intensive programme of trials of the boat, its weapons and other equipment at Holy Loch in Scotland. Sir Charles Craven, the Chairman of Vickers-Armstrongs, wrote to Lieutenant Tomkinson 'It is good news to know that your trials were so successful, and we shall hope to hear very great news of you'.

Many of the initial ship's company stayed with Urge through working up exercises, two war patrols off Norway, passage to Malta and then eighteen Mediterranean war patrols from the besieged island. Leading Seaman Herbert Osborn, who towards the end became 2nd Coxswain,

The original champagne cork and ribbons from the bottle used to launch Urge

was one of those who didn't miss a single patrol. Urge's first two patrols off Norway in January and February 1941 took her just south of the Arctic circle and involved searches for German capital ships, sightings of enemy aircraft and operations with other RN vessels. The blizzards and low temperatures of this initial operational experience for Urge while based in Dundee could not have been in greater contrast to the Mediterranean theatre of war awaiting her. In April, 1941, Urge was ordered to the Mediterranean at short notice. Taking passage down the east coast and then via Portsmouth, Urge sank an enemy ship in the Bay of Biscay and arrived in 'very good spirits' in Gibraltar. Departing a few days later after work on the engines, the submarine arrived in Malta on 6 May, 1941.

Mrs.Myrtle Tomkinson after launching HMS P31 at Barrow, with Lieutenant Tomkinson

HMS H33, Lieutenant Tomkinson's first command in 1940

TELEGRAMS: VICASTRONG, BARROW-IN-FURNESS.   TELEPHONE: 351 BARROW (6 LINES).

Vickers-Armstrongs Limited

Naval Construction Works,
Barrow-in-Furness.

Your Ref.

Our Ref.   Enc.

12ᵉ December, 1940.

Time .1415......

On behalf of VICKERS-ARMSTRONGS LIMITED
I have today handed over J.3386 to the charge of
...... LT. E. P. Tomkinson ....

For VICKERS-ARMSTRONGS LIMITED.

12ᵗ December, 1940.

Time .1415......

On behalf of the BRITISH ADMIRALTY I
have today taken over from Messrs. Vickers-Armstrongs
Ltd., the charge of J.3386.

Signature ..B.P. Tomkinson.

Rank ...... Lieut. R.N.

Lieutenant Tomkinson takes charge of Urge from Vickers-Armstrongs Limited

Urge in the winter of 1940-1, with a full bridge, and crew members on the casing

2

THE 'FIGHTING TENTH' SUBMARINE FLOTILLA

In the Second World War British submarines operated in the Mediterranean from Gibraltar, Malta, Egypt and several other locations. The larger boats from other flotillas including T, P, S and O classes would often pass through or deliver supplies to besieged Malta. For the U class submarines of Malta under the command of Captain GWG Simpson, RN, from September, 1941 designated as the 10th Flotilla, the goal was two-fold – to attack the enemy, including seaborne supplies to German and Italian forces in North Africa, and to defend the island of Malta. Axis forces facing British and Commonwealth armies in the desert depended mainly on shipping for their reinforcements and provisions, and in 1941 Malta-based submarines along with RN surface ships and the RAF achieved notable success attacking this shipping. The flotilla's base centred on the old Lazaretto buildings on Manoel Island, and was known as HMS Talbot. Rock air raid shelters were created beneath the base for personnel, although there was no protection for the submarines themselves as pre-War plans for submarine 'pens' were not completed for reasons of cost; this was to have serious consequences and lead to heavy submarine losses in April, 1942 in particular. Major repairs or refits were undertaken at the Malta dockyard, accessed via the short sea route past Fort St.Elmo to the Grand Harbour.

HMS Talbot: The Lazaretto buildings, Manoel Island, base of the 10th Submarine Flotilla

In making their attacks, submarines such as Urge faced danger at sea across a wide spectrum of enemy opposition, ranging from heavy enemy warships, lighter escort vessels, E boats ('Enemy' boats, a term used for fast motor torpedo boats), U boats (submarines), minefields, coastal defences and aircraft. Enemy fighters, bombers and seaplanes were a constant danger at sea, where the shallow and clear waters of the Mediterranean meant Urge could easily be spotted and attacked when near the surface, or her torpedoes sighted and evaded. To add to the threat of the enemy, Urge's torpedoes failed to run properly on at least three occasions, once forcing her to the surface in full view of her opponents with a torpedo smoking in its tube before being shaken clear. On two other occasions Urge's own torpedoes had faults which caused them to circle and then explode violently beneath her.

A depth charge explodes

Urge's first experience of enemy depth charges in the initial Mediterranean patrol was shocking and disturbing. An officer who served in other 10th Flotilla submarines, Captain MLC Crawford, gave a sense of what it was like when the enemy escorts counter-attacked as a submarine which had fired torpedoes tried to creep away – 'of course the enemy is rushing around trying to find you. You hear their propellers above you and you fall silent. They can pick up anything with their hydrophones. When they drop their depth charges, you wait and wait for the crash to come. You brace and suddenly a great explosion goes off. Lights go out, things crash to the

Urge (on the right) alongside Upholder (left, bulbous bows), December, 1941

floor and you just hope it wasn't too close.'. Some explosions around Urge were so close they physically hurled sailors across the submarine. An SBS commando on board Urge during a heavy depth charging summed up the experience as 'appalling'. Lieutenant-Commander Tomkinson and his team never lost their intense duel with the enemy escort ships, avoiding hundreds of depth charges over many months.

On their return to besieged Malta after demanding patrols the submariners were still in intense danger. At times, Urge had to wait at sea while watching with concern as the island was bombed. Enemy fighters and bombers were a hazard to a submarine leaving or arriving or simply moored or moving around the base. The submariners themselves were faced with air attack in harbour, and like their Maltese friends often had to spend long periods in rock shelters or risk their lives by being above ground. Travel around the island could be lengthy, tiring and hazardous. On several occasions on their return to base after patrol Urge's officers and men found their accommodation destroyed by bombing, their possessions including letters from home lying amid the rubble. Urge's crew continually lost close friends both through enemy action at sea and through bombing in Malta. By April, 1942 the damage caused throughout 1941 was intensifying and the position was particularly desperate. Submarines had to dive out at sea between patrols to avoid systematic enemy bombing of the harbour. Submariners began to find themselves alternating between the confined space of the patrolling submarine and that of the caves which were underground shelters from bombing at the base. They longed to see greenery or the comforts of home.

Rationing pervaded most activities in Malta, although generally the submariners ate reasonably. In part this was because Captain Simpson established a small farm within the bounds of the base, which supplemented the endless tinned food with some fresh provisions until it was destroyed by enemy bombs in Spring, 1942. Each submarine had responsibility for particular animals – as well as providing vital sustenance, the characters among them and their antics provided light relief. At sea, little of the food was fresh, and the effects of a closely confined environment in the submarine without sunlight and the particular violence of depth charging affected health. Many coped with minor injuries or ailments sustained or worsened by the operational conditions. On patrol it was the responsibility of the Commanding

U class submarine of Urge's type, alongside the Lazaretto. Note the raised large search and small attack periscopes

Officer (CO) and the Coxswain (the Chief Petty Officer or CPO) to attend to medical matters.
In the Mediterranean and other operational areas, British submarines dived by day, and usually only

A German parachute mine explodes over Manoel Island (U class submarine visible on the left)

surfaced at night to recharge batteries and take in fresh air, a process often interrupted by sudden diving stations to avoid enemy activity. In summer, the heat was frequently so intense sweat poured off the submariners as they worked or even just rested; in winter, the experience of storms on the surface at night in a small submarine like Urge was uncomfortable and often dangerous, causing risks, strain and damage to boat and sailors alike. The controls of the small U class boats required careful handling, and mistakes or accidents could be fatal. These dangers were particularly acute when making attacks on heavily escorted convoys, or landing special forces or agents on enemy coasts.

As the months of action went on, every member of Urge's crew had to deal not only with the violence and difficulties of their patrolling or besieged environments but prolonged absence from loved ones. Letters and recollections show their longing to be with their families. They also show that morale and the fighting spirit of the submarine was high, with all ranks having a pride in their achievements. However, Lieutenant-Commander Tomkinson and Urge's ship's company were like most of their fellow submariners - whilst they were pleased with their successes, they saw them primarily as a way to end the War which was threatening them and their families as quickly as possible. It is difficult to generalise about the views of several dozen people, evolving over months of intense combat, but there seemed to be a growing reluctance to portray their work or wartime existence as any kind of glorious adventure. They knew all too well it was not.

Captain Simpson was well regarded, and the 10th Flotilla contained many effective commanding officers ('CO's) and submarines. The most successful was HMS Upholder, with whom Urge had a close comradeship. The two captains of these submarines, Lieutenant-Commander MD Wanklyn and

Lieutenant-Commander Tomkinson, were good friends, two officers who Captain Simpson later said 'set an example for all of us'. A later CO, Alastair Mars, remembered that these two COs were 'admired by all in a way that set them at the top…'. The broadcaster Commander Anthony Kimmins came out to Malta in late 1941 and reported on the experiences of the submarines there, being particularly struck by the friendship between the 'ace submarine captains' of Upholder and Urge - 'So different to look at… But both brilliantly clever, both quiet and retiring, both with a lovely sense of humour, and both with identical outlooks on the job they were now doing'. Another successful officer who held submarine command in Malta at this time was Lieutenant Arthur Hezlet (later Vice-Admiral Sir Arthur Hezlet). He later drew attention to a category of submarine captains - and by implication crews - who provided 'indirect leadership of their brother captains by their performance on patrol', stating that 'At the height of the Mediterranean campaign, Lieutenant-Commander MD Wanklyn and Lieutenant-Commander EP Tomkinson set a splendid example'. These two officers' wives were also friends, keeping in contact as the news of Upholder's and Urge's successes began to make headlines.

Although names like Upholder, Urge, and others such as Utmost, Upright and Unbeaten became prominent at this time, all 10th Flotilla boats worked closely together and many of them shared longstanding friendships. In October, 1941 Admiral Sir Max Horton, the Flag Officer Submarines (or head of the RN Submarine Service), visited the 10th Flotilla in Malta. Pictures from the visit show him addressing the whole flotilla as well as meeting with the COs. Admiral Horton had a two hour discussion alone with Lieutenant-Commanders Tomkinson and Wanklyn to discuss their attack techniques. Admiral Horton was a legendary figure, and it would have been a high point for Urge's crew when he reviewed the submarine during his visit.

Lt-Cdr EP Tomkinson (left), Lt-Cdr MD Wanklyn (right), Malta, December, 1941

German Messerschmitt Bf 109 fighters, which were among the aircraft which attacked the British submarines

Admiral Sir Max Horton addressing the 10th Flotilla, HMS Talbot, October, 1941. Lt-Cdr Tomkinson is the tallest officer on the right

The 10th Flotilla submariners listening to Admiral Horton, the head of the RN Submarine Service, October, 1941

Admiral Sir Max Horton (left); Captain GWG Simpson (centre); Lt Cdr EP Tomkinson (right). Left behind Ad Horton is Hugh Mackenzie; left behind Capt Simpson is Ian McGeoch; left behind Edward Tomkinson is David Wanklyn, then in front of him Johnny Wraith.

3

EDWARD PHILIP TOMKINSON

Notwithstanding all the challenges, Urge was a successful, resilient and according to later letters a happy boat. As CO, Lieutenant-Commander Edward Tomkinson RN, was described by Captain Simpson as a 'master of his profession' and 'an outstanding personality with high intelligence, charm and humour', adding 'His leadership and ability have made Urge outstandingly successful, the ship's company work as an enthusiastic team.'.

EP Tomkinson, aged 14, passport photograph for visit to Gibraltar 1926

Edward Philip Tomkinson was born on 22 September, 1911, the younger son of Robert Edward and Beatrice Lucy Tomkinson. From Stubbington House School he went to Dartmouth Royal Naval College in 1925, and from January, 1929 was a Cadet and Midshipman in HMS Repulse. After Lieutenant's courses he was a Sub-Lieutenant in HMS Frobisher before joining the Submarine Service in 1933. He then served in HMS L69, HMS Seahorse, and HMS Thames (including time in Malta as part of Mediterranean service) before becoming first lieutenant of Undine. After command of H33, and during his command of Urge, he was promoted from Lieutenant to Lieutenant-Commander on 1st October, 1941.

Two fellow submarine veterans, each of whom went on to lead the RN Submarine Service as Flag Officer Submarines at different times after the War, later gave recollections of Lieutenant-Commander Tomkinson:

"Tommo' Tomkinson was, by any account, a very remarkable man; large of stature, friendly, overflowing with high spirits and vitality, his intelligence, knowledge and vision were outstanding. Never at a loss for words, nor slow to speak his mind, he also invariably saw the lighter side of things and could be guaranteed to introduce a jovial note into the most serious problem or outlook. His cheerful contribution to life reached everywhere in Blockhouse. I believe his qualities of leadership ranked among the finest ever produced by the submarine service, his friendship was a blessing I treasured. As war looked more and more inevitable, his tongue-in-cheek, light-hearted summing up of how we should meet it, 'No medals,

HMS Repulse, on board which EP Tomkinson was a Midshipman

no tombstones', became our catchphrase.' Vice Admiral Sir Hugh Mackenzie (The Sword of Damocles)

'Tall and robust, with a long face and a friendly expression, 'Tommo' was one of the best officers of his seniority…Tomkinson, whom I knew so well and whose activities I had followed closely, should in my view have been awarded the Victoria Cross – preferably before he was lost.' Vice Admiral Sir Ian McGeoch (An Affair of Chances)

At 6 ft 4 inches Lieutenant-Commander Tomkinson was one of Britain's tallest commanders, in one of the smallest submarines. He was the reigning Royal Navy & Royal Marines Golf Champion throughout the Second World War having won the title in 1939, as well as holding the Somerset County and other golf titles. Ian McGeoch remembered him as wearing his successes lightly and having a pronounced sense of humour.

HMS Thames diving out of Marsamxett Harbour, Malta, May 1936, Tigne Point behind (EP Tomkinson image)

EP Tomkinson as Sub-Lieutenant; RN & RM Golf Society Champion, 1939; Relaxing before the War

In 1986 CET Warren remembered the then Lieutenant Tomkinson's approach from a crew member's perspective when he served with him as a leading stoker working on the build for and in Undine: 'Not only was he one of the great submarine commanders of the Second World War, but he was a real gentleman in all meanings of the word…Tommo was patient, explained everything and listened to any suggestions, he never dictated, it was a team effort.' Warren suggested that the ability fully to involve and work with senior ratings was an essential skill which not all submarine officers had. Lieutenant-Commander Tomkinson's strength in giving training to others was reflected in senior officer's appraisals, along with keenness, cheerfulness, hard work, willingness to take responsibility, loyalty to superiors, tact towards and interest in subordinates (including through a shared interest in sport) and a 'fund of common sense'. In April, 1941 Captain JS Roper of the 9th Submarine Flotilla stated as follows:

'I find it difficult to avoid the use of superlatives in assessing this officer. He exhibits to a marked degree all the officer-like qualities considerably in advance of his years and seniority. An outstanding example of the finest type of Naval Officer.' (Admiral Horton added: 'Concur. A v. fine type of S/M C.O.')

Edward Philip Tomkinson and Myrtle Alice nee Land on their wedding day, 9 April, 1940

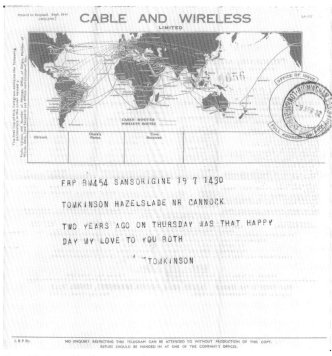

CABLE AND WIRELESS
LIMITED

FRP BM454 SANSORIGINE 19 7 1430

TOMKINSON HAZELSLADE NR CANNOCK

TWO YEARS AGO ON THURSDAY WAS THAT HAPPY
DAY MY LOVE TO YOU BOTH

' 'TOMKINSON

One of the last cables from EP Tomkinson to Mrs.Tomkinson, from war torn Malta, to mark their second wedding anniversary, 9 April, 1942

In 1986 former submarine CO Lieutenant-Commander Richard Raikes wrote to the Assistant Director of the RN Submarine Museum Gus Britton (who had himself served in HMS Uproar, formerly P31, during the War) with some opinions of characters he knew well in the Second World War. Lieutenant-Commander Raikes' summary of Lieutenant-Commander Tomkinson read as follows:

"Tommo' to everyone. A larger-than-life character who enjoyed life to the full. He radiated confidence, because he had great faith in his own ability, though this was very far short of conceit...He led, quite unconsciously, by sheer example. He was a splendid messmate and an inspiring captain who might well have become the greatest of them all.'

Throughout 1941-2 Lieutenant-Commander Tomkinson suffered from back pain, which was at times severe. When he returned from patrol he had to travel through the air raids to various hospitals for regular (often daily) treatment, and was incapacitated and hospitalised by the injury for a short time in August, 1941. He was however determined to continue in command, and had the problem under control to some extent by 1942.

Captain Simpson summarised in 1942 that Lieutenant-Commander Tomkinson 'proved his sterling qualities under exacting conditions of active service...I consider that he is marked for high rank...'

At the time of Lieutenant-Commander Tomkinson's death he was 30 years old.

4

HMS URGE'S SHIP'S COMPANY

The CO of a 1940s submarine had a major impact on the character of the boat, and was the only person with a full picture of what was going on. Often he had to take decisions in an instant and under pressure, and they were his and his alone. In doing so he had great authority and responsibility, but as one successful submarine commander later emphasised:

'…no man relies more completely upon each and every member of his crew. A good submarine crew is far more than a team; they are as near as possible, during attack, a single composite body using the CO as their eye and director'. (Rear Admiral Ben Bryant, Submarine Command)

Writing in 1965, the naval historian Captain Donald Macintyre described Urge's 'splendid fighting submariners' as a 'superlative crew [who] had also built up a brilliant reputation'.

Chief Petty Officer Charley Jackman was Coxswain of Urge from April 1941, at which time he was already a veteran of submarine warfare with awards for service in another submarine. He was praised by Urge's CO for his leadership and positive influence, and Captain Simpson said of CPO Jackman:

'In URGE's fine ship's company one rating stands out with a record that must be for all time exceptional. Chief Petty Officer Jackman began hostilities as [Coxswain of another boat] and in that submarine had attacked enemy vessels in the North Sea on over 20 occasions with a large measure of success. Jackman had been in action during this war well over 40 times against all types of enemy ships.'

CPO Charley Jackman   *PO Henry Watts*   *LS Herbert Osborn*

ERA Eric Varley

Lg Signalman Eric Law

LS Laurence Groves

CPO Jackman was one of several ratings who had already seen action in other vessels. PO Henry Watts had already been mentioned in despatches for submarine service, ERA Eric Varley had served on an aircraft carrier including time in Arctic waters, and Leading Signalman Eric Law had seen action in the destroyer HMS Eskimo off Norway. Leading Seaman Laurence Groves was one of those who had served with Lieutenant-Commander Tomkinson before, in HMS Thames in the mid-1930s. In general it was the senior ratings had the greatest length of service, but many others such as Stoker Albert Bryant had a positive influence through their long experience and character.

The April 1941 order for Urge to head overseas had been sudden and led to rushed goodbyes for all the crew. First Lieutenant Malcolm Poole had been married only three weeks before leaving. He excelled

Lt Malcolm Poole with wife Josie

Lt John Ransome

Lt David Allen

in his demanding role and had the submarine made it to Alexandria he would have flown to the UK to take the Commanding Officer's Qualifying Course. CERA Charles Toms had been with Urge from the beginning and led maintainance of engines and generators in challenging conditions. His role, assisted by two ERAs and the stokers, was like so many others always critical operationally and would also have been crucial in the difficult refit work in the Malta dockyards which occurred amid heavy bombing in February and March, 1942. Petty Officer Henry Watts (in charge of torpedoes) and Stoker Petty Officer William Ashford also led key teams. Lieutenant Allen was the armaments officer, and under the CO's watchful eye from the bridge he also led sailors assisting the special forces and agents leaving and re-joining the submarine.

When not in action there was still plenty of work to do. Accounts describe the working shift – an ERA and stokers in the engine room, the helmsman, ASDIC operator, different ratings working variously on the pumps, cooling machinery, torpedo tubes, electrical testing, a Petty Officer of the watch, duty

PO Tel Peter Wiseman

LS Jesse Norris

Tel Henry Twist

ERA, messenger, spare hand, officer of the watch, and (if the submarine was on the surface) lookouts. Often crew members would have a variety of roles. For example, Leading Signalman Eric Law's role involved communicating with other vessels and shore stations as well as being a bridge lookout. For this reason the signalman was often first on the bridge after the CO when surfacing. Peter Wiseman as PO Telegraphist not only led the wireless transmission work but undertook many other tasks such as recording the number and range of depth charges as they exploded near the submarine. In the small U class boats there was no full time cook and an Able Seaman undertook the role. Like Eric Law, Able Seaman John O'Neill was one of the sharp team of lookouts, and also operated the ASDIC set (for listening underwater) when they were submerged. The reports, citations and letters show only some of the many individual contributions.

There was almost no privacy in a cramped 1940s submarine, less in a small U class, and less still when

Lg Stoker Wilfred Lamb

AB Leslie Baxter

Stoker Cyril Brown

commandos, agents or other passengers were embarked. In theory shifts were 2 hours on and 4 hours off at sea, but rest on patrol was often difficult to come by in practice. By contrast, long journeys on passage could be monotonous, with letter writing, conversation, reading and games used to pass the submerged time when not working or training. Lieutenant-Commander Tomkinson constructed rudimentary toys for his daughter, these and similar tasks drew lots of people in, and were a source of amusement and diversion, as were long chats about home. When at sea for longer periods on patrol informal uniforms were often worn and whilst there was still a hierarchy there was less distance between ranks than in larger surface ships. In action the emphasis was on doing jobs well rather than saluting and other formalities. There were three small basins, one for officers, one for Petty Officers, and one for other ratings, although there wasn't much need for shaving on patrol and most people would have sported beards at one time or another. A letter from Able Seaman Leslie Baxter in November, 1941 told his sister that he was 'bewhiskered' and not washing for two weeks at a time or particularly enjoying the foul air in the submarine, to which would have been added the pervasive smell of diesel and oil.

The team trusted their CO and each other and this enabled them to thrive under the considerable pressures they faced. They were mostly young, predominantly in their 20s, with the oldest believed to be 38. Overall, they had cheerful and even-tempered outlooks combined with professional, personal and sporting success. Many crew members enjoyed sports such as rugby, PO Peter Wiseman and Stoker Cyril Brown being among those with many cups to their names. When the wartime conditions allowed, which in 1941 they sometimes did despite the bombing, the crew relished team games

Casing awash at sea (pre-War image by EP Tomkinson on HMS Thames)

which all took part in. Naval successes had a very positive effect on morale, as did letters and news of families from home. Bad weather was highly unpopular with the ship's company, as was anything which delayed or interrupted letters from home. Amid the most extreme operational and military perils, news of wives, girlfriends, children and other family were of paramount concern, and wedding anniversaries and thoughts of good times past and to come were always at the front of minds.

Some crew members went on to other things, and the process of their replacements settling in could have operational implications for the submarine as a whole. At least two attacks failed due to new crew members making mistakes. In both cases those crew members quickly went on to be highly successful and strong members of the ship's company, wholly dependable in their roles.

Their names do not appear in this book, but at least two people left Urge due to 'nervous strain' after heavy depth charging, and there was the occasional person who Lieutenant-Commander Tomkinson, CPO Jackman or the senior rates decided was not the right 'fit' for various reasons. In one particularly stressful patrol where one of Urge's torpedoes lodged in its tube, toxic gas from its smoking motor caused dangerous fumes and the submarine to lighten and break surface in front of the enemy. Quick action ordered by the CO freed the torpedo, but after the heavy depth charging Urge took in retribution one crew member paced part of the submarine reciting the Lord's Prayer for 'some time'. Captain Simpson highlighted this to superior officers as an example of 'the serious strain on personnel attacking heavily escorted convoys'. They noted this 'gruelling experience' and the 'very high standard of skill, courage and discipline throughout the submarine.'. Every member of the ship's company who was lost had stood the course supremely, but no-one pretended it was easy. It cannot be known whether all of them would have returned home with the same perspectives they left with, had they survived. Able Seaman Baxter felt like a 'proper little blitz hound' amid the dangers of the 'daring deep sea domains' when writing soon after one very challenging patrol. Several spoke of hair turning grey amid the blasts. Most were extraordinarily stoic, Leading Stoker Richard Wildman's parents later relating that 'He never complained and he said he liked his job very much'. Able Seaman John Parkinson's widow said 'My husband was always cheerful, and often talked of their successes at sea, [of] which he seemed very proud.'. Writing to his wife towards the end, while Lieutenant-Commander Tomkinson talked of the impact of months of depth charging and the huge explosions of bombs and parachute mines dropped by the Luftwaffe, he was resolutely clear – 'we can take it'.

Loading a torpedo in a confined space

As Mrs.Parkinson said, there was considerable pride in the submarine's achievements, and as was the practice for successful British submarines Urge flew a skull and crossbones Jolly Roger flag on return to harbour. The ship's badge depicting two interlocking spurs was displayed in the control room. For special occasions like the birth of the CO's daughter Bridget in July, 1941, flags flew from Urge and a bottle of beer each was made available for a toast. Preparing for an inspection or visit from senior officers or other VIPs involved a lot of work by the crew. The high standards expected within Urge were undoubtedly demanding, but they bred a confidence which extended beyond appearances into operational effectiveness, health and the outlook of the whole ship's company. Demands and dangers were also tempered by a strong sense of humour which prevailed within the submarine, and this blend of professionalism and an ability to lighten difficult situations was critical for both morale and success. Time and again, the families of Urge crew members, for example that of Leading Stoker Wilfred Lamb, as well as others in all roles, still recount today this sense of humour alongside resolution and skill when describing those they lost.

Many of the crew's family members had toured the submarine when it was in harbour in the UK prior to leaving for the Mediterranean. Leading Signalman Eric Law's father was Chief Yeoman of Signals Charles Law DSM, a veteran of the First World War. He later described to Mrs.Tomkinson his visit to

Stoker PO William Ashford *Stoker Joseph McMillan* *Stoker Marcus Stanger*

see his son and Urge when the submarine put in to the naval base of Scapa Flow in Scotland where he was serving in early 1941:

'I had the pleasure of meeting your dear husband when I went on board the Urge on her first visit to Scapa [Flow] and certainly had a good half hour chat with him. It struck me very forceably of the wonderful morale and good humour of the crew when I went down below (between decks), Captain, Officers and Crew 100 per cent sailors and made me feel very proud, and admire the Submarine Service.'

Mrs.Ethel Bryant, widow of Stoker Albert Bryant, remembered her own tour of Urge when she had been at Barrow, and her husband's pride as he showed her around. 'He was such a good husband, and he loved the Navy. He was always talking about the Submarine, and always looked on the bright side of things'.

Lieutenant-Commander Tomkinson and the leaders in his team in Urge had trained the ship's company to high efficiency. Relatively few crew members left the boat, and when they did their replacements were thoroughly trained up to reach the prevailing standards.

Detail of 10th Flotilla crews featuring members of Urge ship's company

Living space in a submarine (note bread stored above)

5

ACHIEVEMENTS AND RECORD

The battleship Vittorio Veneto, torpedoed by Urge in the Straits of Messina, 14 December, 1941

The head of the RN Submarine Service said in May, 1942 that Lieutenant-Commander Tomkinson's 'courage, leadership and great skill were second to none in the Submarine Service either in this War or the last…his loss to the nation is irreparable and bitterly felt' (Admiral Sir Max Horton). In March, 1943, Admiral Horton's successor wrote to Mrs.Tomkinson that 'Your

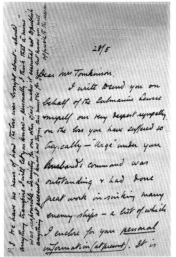

Letter from Admiral Horton to Mrs.Tomkinson, May, 1942

The Vittorio Veneto on 14 December, 1941 very shortly after Urge's torpedo strike under the port side of the aft turret; the stern is low in the water due to flooding and damage

Urge's hit put the Vittorio Veneto out of action for several months (the battleship is seen here firing a broadside)

Italian cruiser Giovanni Delle Bande Nere, torpedoed by Urge on 1 April, 1942

Bande Nere at sea

husband's name will live for ever in the Submarine Service' (Admiral Sir Claud Barry).

In July, 1945, Admiral Barry's successor described Lieutenant-Commander Tomkinson as 'one of the most outstanding submarine captains in the proud history of the Submarine Branch' (Admiral Sir George Creasy).

These remarks also reflect positively on each person who served on and lost their lives in Urge. Lieutenant-Commander Tomkinson and his ship's company will be remembered for sinking the enemy cruiser Giovanni Delle Bande Nere, and for achieving the unique distinction for an RN submarine of torpedoing an enemy battleship (the Vittorio Veneto) in addition to that cruiser sinking. Sinking the Bande Nere with two torpedo hits at a range of 5000 yards removed a threat to the RN which had caused considerable casualties to the Allies through effective minelaying, and in the Second Battle of Sirte. The discovery of the wreck of the Bande Nere itself by the Italian navy in early 2019 is a reminder that there was heavy loss of life on both sides. The Italian warship sank in a matter of minutes after the second torpedo struck.

Bande Nere

Urge also had multiple successes against enemy merchant vessels. This included sinking the Franco Martelli, at 10,800 tons this ship was one of the largest tankers sunk by an RN submarine. Such vessels were not easy to sink due to their watertight compartments, and a further torpedo was needed after the initial hit. The tanker had been closely tracked in enemy ports by the Special Operations Executive (SOE) due to its importance and value to the enemy. Ian McGeoch recalled later: 'As a 'spare commanding officer' I was taking passage to Malta with Tommo in the Urge

Bande Nere on 1 April, 1942; the ship is breaking in two and sinking after two hits from Urge's torpedoes, as seen from an escorting destroyer

when he torpedoed the large blockade-running tanker Franco Martelli; she was carrying fuel for the U boats and her loss was a serious blow to the enemy.' A number of other merchant ships were also

The tanker Franco Martelli, torpedoed by Urge in the Bay of Biscay, 18 April, 1941

The transport ship Aquitania, torpedoed by Urge near Sicily, 27 August, 1941

The transport ship Marigola, torpedoed by Urge off Tunisia, 22 October, 1941

torpedoed in the Mediterranean by Urge.

In July, 1941 Urge was the second of a three submarine team which pioneered a new route for British submarines through the notoriously dangerous enemy declared minefield QBB 65 south of Sicily. The submarines were required to provide screening against Italian fleet interference in the Malta convoy Operation Substance, as part of which they tested the route. HMS Utmost went first, and was followed by Urge, then followed by Upholder, a trio Captain Simpson described as his 'best team'. The courage shown by these three boats saved many lives, as no submarines were thought to have been lost on this route thereafter.

In one patrol in August, 1941 Urge attacked an enemy convoy and, as has been related, had a close escape when a malfunctioning torpedo jammed in the tube, causing the submarine to surface. Later in the same patrol Lieutenant Tomkinson and Urge's crew attacked another convoy, at one point diving from periscope depth to 50 feet to allow an enemy destroyer to pass overhead, before returning to periscope depth to resume the attack. Commanders (including Admiral Horton) agreed when a senior Admiralty officer stated: '...I should like to record it as my opinion that Tomkinson, in his second attack, gave one of the most outstanding displays of courage yet given by a submarine CO in this war.' Such official assessments reflected on the whole ship's company involved in these attacks.

Only with the release of official files decades after the War could it be appreciated that Urge also had a pioneering role working with the SBS (the Special Boat Service, or at that time, Section). This included landing commandos who blew up enemy trains on two occasions, including the first time such a success was achieved by the SBS. Enemy trains carried munitions, so

Urge's 'Jolly Roger' flag. The daggers denote special missions

destroying them reduced the flow of bombs falling on Malta and the casualties they caused, as well as tying up enemy forces protecting the lines. In this work Lieutenant-Commander Tomkinson worked closely with Captain Robert 'Tug' Wilson DSO*, an SBS pioneer, and SBS commandos were aboard for at least 4 of Urge's 18 Mediterranean patrols. The submarine was also called upon to land special agents in hazardous circumstances for the Special Intelligence Service, or SIS (MI6). Twice Lieutenant-Commander Tomkinson and his team's skill enabled the submarine to avoid traps set by the enemy during special missions of this kind. Very sadly, on one of those occasions enemy fire killed Sub Lieutenant Brian Lloyd who was courageously closing the shore in a folbot (folding boat, or canoe) to collect a

secret agent. It later emerged that the agent had been captured by the enemy. Urge's Jolly Roger carried six dagger symbols, each denoting special operations.

Urge's prominent 12 pounder deck gun was probably used in action on only one occasion. In an action with an armed merchant ship in March, 1942 the enemy ship was chased and damaged by Urge using both the deck gun and also machine gun fire from a Lewis gun mounted on the conning tower. However, the enemy returned fire and water thrown up from the near miss of an enemy shell soaked those on Urge's bridge. Lieutenant-Commander Tomkinson decided to dive rather than risk his boat in a duel, as a damaged submarine was unable to dive and would have been very vulnerable on the

Sub-Lieutenant Brian Lloyd, lost on special mission, 2 October, 1941

surface. U class submarines of Urge's specific type had a relatively ineffective, older 12 pounder gun re-used from World War One or even before. These had been rushed into service again in 1940, but were being replaced in later submarines by a more modern 3 inch gun firing a 20 pound shell which like the 4 inch guns carried by larger British submarines had greater effect. There were other reasons for Lieutenant-Commander Tomkinson to be sparing in the use of the deck gun. First, in 1941-2 enemy air power in the Mediterranean was stronger than later in the War, and time on the surface to use an underpowered gun was known to carry disproportionate risk. Secondly, at this time the submarines were focused on targeting large enemy vessels (of which there were still a good quantity) and were reluctant to reveal their position for smaller gun targets unless, perhaps, they had used all their torpedoes. This tactical position altered later in the War when some of these factors changed, but Urge had been lost by then.

On a number of occasions Urge's torpedoes missed their target, and the various causes are interesting. As related, one German U boat and other enemy vessels almost certainly owed their survival to faults in the torpedoes supplied to Urge amid difficult base conditions in late 1941. The U boat was U-331, whose lookouts saw only one torpedo track, so it appears the others would have been on target but for their malfunction. One of Urge's faulty torpedoes (or 'circlers' as they were known) was heard to pass down the port side – an 'unpleasant sound' – and exploded underneath her. One of the crew made a wry

Passing a folbot through a submarine's torpedo loading hatch

comment on this shocking situation, which Lieutenant-Commander Tomkinson approved of so much he put it into his patrol report – 'As one of the ship's company remarked, 'when we have these Mk.VIII two star torpedoes on board, we had better point our stern at the enemy if we want a hit." Urge's bad luck with faulty torpedoes had tragic consequences, as U-331 escaped and went on to sink the British battleship HMS Barham with heavy loss of life a short time later.

In the 14th December, 1941 attack on the enemy fleet, Urge's torpedoes had been on target to hit the battleship Littorio as well as Vittorio Veneto, but the former's lookouts spotted them and took evasive action. Aircraft and lookouts in several warships and convoys saw and avoided torpedoes from Urge which were running true on several occasions. In March, 1942 an enemy merchant vessel was alerted to Urge's presence by the explosion of charges the submarine's commandos had laid on a railway line, which meant torpedoes had to be fired from long range which compromised success. Other torpedoes passed underneath targets or even apparently failed to explode on striking them. Errors could be made of course, and sometimes these led to failed attacks, but there were usually other reasons for Urge's torpedoes missing targets.

A U class submarine in Malta loading a torpedo

Anthony Kimmins had observed that each of Lieutenant-Commanders Wanklyn and Tomkinson were calculating COs who thought out situations before committing themselves, and avoided impetuous decisions. In September, 1941 Captain Simpson called his COs together and informed them of a plan to sail within an hour to attack an enemy convoy, news of which had just been received. He stated that if any CO felt their submarine was not ready they should say so and they could be counted out. Lieutenant-

Firing a Lewis machine gun at sea (pre-War image by EP Tomkinson on HMS Thames)

Commander Tomkinson took this opportunity to say that he felt that Urge was not ready. A letter to his wife reveals that he made this decision because two of his three officers were incapacitated with fevers; the remaining junior officer was comparatively new, and there were likely to have been other illnesses or absences among a crew that had endured 46 depth charges on their previous patrol. As CO he was fit, and able to go, but given the option by Simpson he followed his instincts not to risk his crew in an unprepared submarine compromised by absences due to illness. (In the event, the mission was a considerable success, with two large sinkings for Upholder.)

The results of attacks were not always known at the time, as submarines usually needed to begin their submerged escape from counter attacks below periscope depth immediately after firing torpedoes. This meant moving as quickly and silently as possible away from the area where the torpedo tracks began at the point of firing, a point often visible to the enemy. A myriad of underwater sounds could be heard as each side's weapons were deployed and detonated, and it wasn't always clear what these sounds were and whether torpedoes had hit. Lieutenant-Commander Tomkinson used variations of depth, speed, and direction as well as prevailing weather, physical conditions and silent routines to evade enemy counter attacks. On one occasion he judged that enemy attackers

A U class submarine's engine room

were so close to sinking Urge that to shake off continued detection he delayed using the motors to stabilise a dive the submarine was making. The boat silently glided below the designed depth limit by 28 feet, but the enemy lost contact, and Urge survived both the depth and the enemy to fight another day.

CPO Jackman (left) and PO Tel Wiseman (right) in seagoing clothes (pre-War images)

In wartime conditions some British submarines mistook Allied craft for foes and there were a number of 'friendly fire' incidents or mistakes in attacking ships which should have been given safe passage. Tragically, some British submarines sank enemy ships which, unknown to them, had large numbers of British prisoners of war on board, many of whom lost their lives. Thankfully, Urge was not involved in any incidents of this kind.

During her initial patrols in the North Sea Urge faced German naval and air opposition. In one of these patrols the submarine was diverted from a pre-planned mission to intercept enemy shipping off Norway to search for the German heavy cruiser Hipper. Once in the Mediterranean, both German and Italian units were faced, the latter containing some particularly effective anti-submarine units which accounted for many British submarines.

6

HMS URGE'S LOSS

Malta's desperate situation under siege and air attack in April, 1942 meant that the 10th Flotilla's continued use of its base on Manoel Island became untenable. Most submarines had been destroyed or evacuated, many in a damaged state, and by the end of the month following losses or evacuation of other boats Urge was the longest serving survivor of the last five U classes operating. By now the submarines had to dive by day, either risking bombs by being submerged in harbour or being taken to sea to submerge during

daylight hours before coming back at night for maintenance and re-arming. Marxashett Creek in front of the Lazaretto buildings of HMS Talbot was systematically bombed by the German Stukas, Mcsserschmitts, Junkers and Dorniers and the Italian air force. Marks left by cannon and machine gun fire are still visible in the walls of the Lazaretto building today, but the heavier bombs including parachute mines caused the greatest damage.

One estimate suggested 6,727 tons of bombs were dropped on Malta in April, of which nearly half fell on the dockyard and surrounding areas. Lieutenant-Commander

Destruction caused by air raids at HMS Talbot, May 1942

Tomkinson's letters to his wife talk of the 'very severe blitzing' which was making the submariners' existence virtually untenable. Even the sailors' rest camps were being shot up, and sleep was difficult to achieve. As he and others thought of family and home, they particularly resented seeing enemy planes target civilians in Malta, sights which made them more determined to win the War against the regimes they faced. In one letter to his mother at this time Lieutenant-Commander Tomkinson related 'They certainly turned the heat on alright' but amid these arduous times he was able to say 'My boys are all very well and the boat seems to just keep on going thanks to a lot of hard work.'.

The 10th Flotilla's submarines faced almost certain destruction in their own base. At this time, a scheme was proposed to rotate different crews on patrol around the submarines so that in theory the boats

Detail of a Luftwaffe map featuring Manoel Island

could spend more time at sea. Lieutenant-Commander Tomkinson strongly resisted this idea, gravely concerned about the impact it would have had on Urge's crew and their safety and operational effectiveness. He suggested that it was preferable for his crew to remain at sea in Urge for long periods rather than have them constantly swapping in and out of different boats which they would not be familiar with. Captain Simpson consulted other COs and it was agreed that this view was correct, so the idea was dropped. Admiral Horton was firmly of the same view as Lieutenant-Commander Tomkinson, articulating that any such rotation scheme would lose 'the espirit de corps engendered in a submarine crew by pride in the individuality of their vessel and of its achievements', and that morale and operations would have been adversely affected.

The enemy was laying minefields to destroy or trap Allied vessels including submarines in Malta, and British minesweeping capability which was so vital for the viability of submarine operations had for a time been effectively destroyed by fighter and bomber attacks. Although submarines were potentially a key defence against a possible invasion of Malta, the RN decided there was no choice but to evacuate the remaining boats of the flotilla to Alexandria on a temporary basis. Lieutenant-Commander Tomkinson's last cable to his wife was sent on 24th April, 1942: 'FIT AND FLOURISHING DO NOT SEND ANY MORE CABLES UNTIL YOU GET ANOTHER FROM ME.'. His last letter of the 62 he had sent since leaving Portsmouth just over a year earlier, dated 26th April, 1942, was as positive as ever, and as

Bernard Gray, War Correspondent

usual, dominated by questions about and thoughts of family and home. Urge's ship's company would have been delighted at the prospect of some respite in Alexandria, albeit they were not heading home just yet. According to an account related to his family, Leading Seaman Jesse Norris was injured but insisted on being carried aboard for the voyage rather than have his comrades sail without him.

Urge sailed for Alexandria at 4.45am on 27th April, 1942. HMS P31 (Lieutenant JBB Kershaw) had sailed 24 hours before, and HMS Porpoise which had brought supplies to Malta followed a couple of days later. What remained of Urge's crew's possessions after the bombing were all on board, crammed into the small submarine along with all manner of equipment. Lieutenant-Commander Tomkinson also agreed to take eleven naval personnel and the well known War Correspondent Bernard Gray to Alexandria as passengers. The naval personnel were submariners from the base, of whom at least one (Leading Seaman Sidney Chamberlain) had been wounded in the bombing raids. Mr.Gray was heading

A Luftwaffe Stuka dive bomber

U class submarine similar to Urge diving (Urge had a W/T folded astern of the conning tower)

to Egypt to cover the desert war, and was well aware that his submarine journey was a dangerous one. Urge had featured in the British press a fair bit, and Mr.Gray was likely to have told a fascinating story of his journey with Lieutenant-Commander Tomkinson and his submariners.

Urge was expected in Alexandria on 6th May, 1942, but never arrived, and was never heard from again. For Captain Simpson and the flotilla this was a 'bitter blow'. He thought it unlikely that Urge would have fallen victim to an enemy aircraft or U boat due to her 'efficient vigilance', and believed a mine was responsible. In fact, we now know that Urge's course took her through the German MT13 minefield which had been laid at night by the Kriegsmarine Third S-Boat (Motor Torpedo Boat) Flotilla on the night of 20th April, 1942, and a mine of this field caused the fatal explosion.

Following Urge becoming overdue, RN authorities in Alexandria waited anxiously for any word from her. The other submarines arrived in a poor state with bomb damage and exhausted and overcrowded occupants but, after many agonising days, eventually it had to be accepted that Urge was not going to

A German mine is laid

German S boat (anti-sweeping mines visible at the stern)

arrive. The naval message below was sent to London:

'NAVAL MESSAGE dated 16th May, 1942
FROM: Commander-in-Chief, Royal Navy, Mediterranean
TO: Admiralty

1. Much regret to report URGE, Lieutenant-Commander TOMKINSON overdue since 6th May and must be considered lost. URGE sailed from MALTA 27th April for passage to ALEXANDRIA. Have no information to show possible cause of loss. S10 is requested to report casualties.
2. Loss of this outstanding submarine and commanding officer is much to be regretted.'

For the 10th Flotilla, the loss of Urge was later spoken of as 'hard to bear', coming soon after the loss of their close friends in Upholder in the middle of April. Captain Simpson anguished as to how it could have been avoided, and mourned:

'The four survivors of our small flotilla felt the loss acutely; it was natural that we all felt that if such olympian exponents of skill and judgement fall, then the odds against survival were slender.'

The mood was also summed up by another successful submarine commander who was at Alexandria at the time, who recalled that Urge "never reached her destination and is thought to have finally succumbed to a mine in the Malta approaches, and so was lost a gallant crew with their exceptionally gifted CO".
(Rear Admiral Sir Anthony Miers, VC)

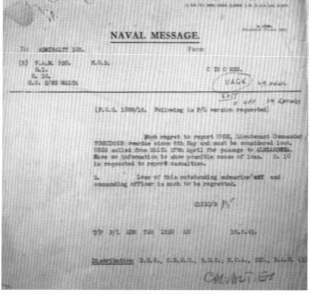

Urge lost: the Commander in Chief's signal to the Admiralty

After 16th May, 1942 official news of the loss started to ripple out, but only to those in the Submarine Service and to next of kin. Families were asked to keep it secret for many months until the announcement was made in September, 1942 that 44 young people in their prime had disappeared in Urge without trace. Each name on the list of those lost was mourned by loved ones in Britain. CPO Jackman's widow Elsie was not alone in later describing the news as 'pretty shattering'. The Jackman family lost another family member only a few days later when CPO Jackman's cousin Leading Stoker James Jackman DSM was lost in Olympus on the same minefield as Urge.

It was not easy for those who were left to carry on the War after losing friends in Urge and other vessels. In July 1942 Lieutenant Jack Kershaw, who had been one of Lieutenant-Commander Tomkinson's closest friends, wrote to Mrs.Tomkinson about her husband:

'Teddy was such a help to me when we first came out to this place and took no end of trouble to give me the benefit of his own vast experience. While we were together life was bearable, but now it is not such fun. However, I feel he would be very annoyed if we moped and did not get on with the job.'

After Urge was lost, in late 1942 Lieutenant-Commander Tomkinson's widow Mrs.Myrtle Tomkinson obtained Admiralty approval to write to all Urge crew next of kin. This was an unusual step at that time, and Mrs.Tomkinson had to overcome Admiralty misgivings about the idea, but she felt it her duty. In December, 1940 she had launched the U class submarine P31 (later Uproar), built at Barrow by the same firm which had constructed Urge. Fate had it that this was the very submarine which had left Malta 24 hours before Urge. Mrs.Tomkinson's father was Commander Charles Land RN, who had been a submariner before the First World War. Although her letters of condolence and the replies from families tell a very sad story, they do affirm that the boat had been a happy one, and all aboard took very great pride in their successes and high standards. These letters were mainly from 1942-3 and were kept by Mrs.Tomkinson. Unseen for many years, today they are once again connecting Urge crew family members.

Mrs.Muriel Toms, widow of CERA Charles Toms, wrote to Mrs.Tomkinson 'My husband always spoke so highly of your husband and often wrote what a happy boat she was. It seems beyond our understanding that this should happen to them – almost on the last lap.'

Lieutenant-Commander Tomkinson's commendations in official reports confirm that he also thought highly of CERA Toms. Mrs.Toms was right, because Urge had been due to return home to the UK in June, 1940, to refit in Blyth, Northumberland, near the homes of several crew members.

Lieutenant David Allen's mother Josephine (whose husband was an Engineer Rear Admiral) spoke of the rapport the ship's company had with each other and their CO. David Allen had written in the highest terms about both, and had commented that Lieutenant-Commander Tomkinson knew the boat 'from A to Z' and had brought Urge out of danger in many difficult situations.

Leading Seaman Jesse Norris' mother said that 'Officers and men on HMS Urge seemed like one big family'; Able Seaman Davison's father said 'My son Robert always spoke of the happiness on his boat and the undying popularity of his commander, his letters were always full of cheerfulness and full of victory.' Stoker Alfred Bryant's wife said 'They were so happy and had every hope of coming home'.

Gordon Selby DSM*, a good friend of CPO Jackman and who had been Upholder's Second Coxwain in 1941-2, wrote of the serious impact of the loss of his Urge friends in 1986. He added that Lieutenant-Commander Tomkinson 'was held in the highest esteem,

The late CPO Jackman's son receives the Bar to his DSM after Urge's loss

both professionally and personally, by everyone who came into contact with him and the loss of "Urge" and "Upholder" within days of one another was a great blow to those of us who were privileged to know the ship's companies of both submarines'.

Many of Urge's ship's company left young children, some of whom they had never seen. Others had the promise of families in the future – 'We know that our dear boy was happy from his letters home. He was to be married on his next leave.' wrote Able Seaman John Rowley DSM's mother Sybil. PO Henry Watts DSM's parents suffered not only his loss but also around the same time that of his brother who had been killed while serving in the Coldstream Guards in Libya. One of the few real comforts for families was the knowledge that those lost in Urge had enjoyed that espirit de corps which Lieutenant-Commander Tomkinson and Admiral Horton had recognised held so much value. Stoker Petty Officer William Ashford DSM's widow, Violet Ashford, wrote to Mrs.Tomkinson: 'You tell me in your letter that your husband thought a lot of his men, well I can tell you that the feeling was sincerely returned. My husband didn't usually indulge in hero worship, but he talked to me often of his commander and the description he gave of him was enough to inspire me with the same confidence in him that my husband had'.

All families found it difficult to cope. One of the few effective ways to do so was to keep busy, and the War continued to make demands of the many bereaved families, of which Urge's were only a small number. Families found it distressing that no personal effects could be sent to them, as these had all been taken with the crew and so were lost with Urge.

Lg Signalman Ronald Leeke

Lg Stoker Samuel Wilkes

The last word in this section must go to Stoker Joseph McMillan's father, who wrote in late 1942 'I may say that the boy liked all the crew of his boat' and summed up:

'I think we can say without regret that they have all done what was asked of them in their duty as part of the Royal Navy, and I think we should all be proud of them for what they have done to save those whom they left at home.'

7

AWARDS, RECOGNITION AND REMEMBRANCE

Submarine awards were made for successes to the boat's leaders and a cross section of the crew. It was accepted, however, that this recognition belonged to the whole crew. Whilst awards were valued, contemporary accounts and veterans indicate that sinkings and most particularly survival had greater currency.

Lt-Cdr Tomkinson's medals: the DSO and Bar was presented to Mrs. Tomkinson by King George VI in 1943

Urge was a highly decorated submarine, crew members being awarded one DSO (Distinguished Service Order), one bar to the DSO, three DSCs (Distinguished Service Cross), one bar to the DSC, 13 DSMs (Distinguished Service Medal), two bars to the DSM, and twelve MIDs (mentions in despatches). A small number of these crew members went on to other submarines where several won further awards. Unfortunately, some of Urge's awards were gazetted after the loss of the recipients, as the official paperwork needed to travel from besieged Malta via Alexandria to London in wartime conditions.

Most of Urge's awards came in 1941. Lieutenant-Commander Tomkinson was awarded a 'double DSO' (ie DSO and Bar) in one gazette for 'outstanding bravery, skill and resolution in successful Submarine patrols', two years' seniority for meritorious war service and a mention in despatches for 'courage, skill and resolution' in command of Urge. Awards to others on Urge were expressed to be for similar services, some of the surviving citations providing more detail of individual contributions.

These awards to Lieutenant-Commander Tomkinson covered the period up to September, 1941. His greatest successes were, however, achieved after this date, and it was intended by Captain Simpson that

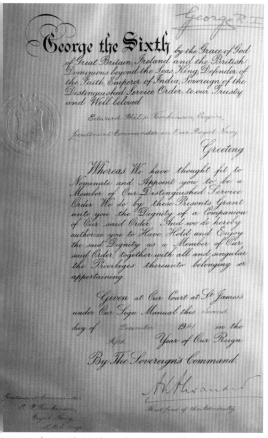

Warrant for Lt-Cdr Tomkinson's DSO signed by AV Alexander, First Lord of the Admiralty

he should receive further awards for them. It is now known that a number of recommendations at the relevant time were never received, as they were destroyed by enemy bombing at the Malta submarine base. This was not realised at the time for several reasons, including ongoing destruction caused by enemy action in Malta and amid the 10th Flotilla's two relocations before returning to Malta. It therefore appears most likely that enemy action not only led to Lieutenant-Commander Tomkinson's death but also deprived him of his final awards, as they could not be considered without the flotilla paperwork.

Captain Simpson later wrote he had told Lieutenant-Commander Tomkinson that by December, 1941 his skill and successes were comparable to VC level, but the CO of Urge had been far more interested in the 'end of the war medal', so he and his crew could get home, and that he 'hated war and despised its rewards'. However, Captain Simpson further made clear in the June, 1942 official report into the loss of Urge that he considered the 10th Flotilla had two COs at VC level, in remarks endorsed by the Commander-in-Chief Mediterranean, when he stated the following concerning Lieutenant-Commanders Wanklyn, VC and Tomkinson:

'Lieutenant-Commander Tomkinson was an outstandingly able leader, whose strict disciplinary methods were mellowed by a great sense of humour, charm and understanding. The chief difference between Tomkinson and Wanklyn was that the former suffered fools less gladly. The determination, forethought and excellent eye of both officers produced results of an equally high order of merit.'

Lieutenant-Commander Tomkinson had been very pleased when his friend Lieutenant-Commander Wanklyn had received the VC in 1941, telling Mrs.Tomkinson that Lieutenant-Commander Wanklyn was clearly the leading ace of the 10th Flotilla. Later, Lieutenant-Commander Wanklyn's widow Elspeth (Betty) voiced the view of many that Urge's CO was expected to receive the flotilla's second VC. After Urge sank the Bande Nere in April, 1942 Mrs.Wanklyn had cabled Mrs.Tomkinson with congratulations, saying 'What will their Lordships give him now?', and as they mourned their losses in August that year wrote 'I expect your Teddy will be given a VC for all his good work…'.

Admiral Hezlet and John Wingate DSC, 10th Flotilla veterans who became submarine historians, were among those who considered that, in the absence of a VC for whatever reason, Lieutenant-

Commander Tomkinson had earned four DSOs, and accordingly would have 'almost certainly' have received two further bars had he survived. The DSO could not be awarded posthumously; in fact, recommendations appear to have been made before the loss, but there is no evidence Lieutenant-Commander Tomkinson's were ever received. Against that background, Admiral Hezlet felt that confusion in wartime conditions was probably responsible for the omission, agreeing with the

Lt-Cdrs David Wanklyn and Edward Tomkinson among the sailors of the 10th Flotilla and SBS commandos

case for a VC: 'Lieutenant-Commander Tomkinson's style of command was second to none. He was always cheerful and ready to get at the enemy.' Another historian and veteran, Gus Britton, wrote of a widespread post-War view that a VC for Urge's achievements had been merited. A similar view is seen in comments from Bill Haines, who had served on Urge in 1941, and summed up the feelings of many when he wrote in 1986 that 'as one enters the Submarine Museum at the top of the stairs there are photos of all VCs, to me there will always be one missing and that's Tommo's.'.

Leading Seaman Jesse Norris and his DSM

CPO Jackman was awarded the DSM and Bar, as well as being mentioned in despatches twice in his career. Several other members of the crew were awarded decorations as well as being mentioned in despatches. Service on Urge earned the campaign medals 1939-45 Star, Africa Star and War Medal (the latter with oak leaves if mentioned in despatches). In addition, the first two patrols and Atlantic passage counted towards entitlement for the Atlantic Star. Some crew members like ERA Eric Varley qualified for the Arctic Star through prior service, although Urge's Norway patrols themselves were a little south of the qualifying area. For pre-War service, CPO Jackman and CERA Toms held the RN Long Service and Good Conduct Medal, and several crew members held the Naval General Service Medal with Palestine clasp.

Chief Engine Room Artificer Charles Toms' medals: DSM, 1939-45 Star, Atlantic Star, Africa Star, 1939-45 War Medal, Naval Long Service and Good Conduct Medal

In 1944 Mrs.Tomkinson donated a stained glass window depicting St.Paul in the chapel at HMS Dolphin in Fort Blockhouse, dedicated to the memory of her husband and the officers and men of Urge. The chapel also contained tributes to CPO Jackman and Urge from Mrs.Jackman and her family. Elsewhere, ERA Eric Varley's parents were jewellers and created silver candlesticks for their local church in memory of him, which are still there today. PO Wiseman's niece continues to treasure a small Urge brooch given to her family by him. Lieutenant-Commander Tomkinson's family still has the original cork from the champagne bottle which launched Urge, mounted on a wooden base with a Vickers-Armstrongs shield, with the original red, white and blue ribbons, now fading.

The Chapel, former HMS Dolphin, Fort Blockhouse, Gosport.

In 1948 the RN Submarine Service named a building at HMS Dolphin after Urge. The then Captain Ben Bryant, as commanding officer of Dolphin at the time, wrote to Mrs.Tomkinson that 'the blocks are being named after submarines who distinguished themselves in World War II, and of course URGE has a block named after her.'. The historian Captain Macintyre said of Urge in 1971 'this was a submarine which under the command of Lieutenant EP Tomkinson had gained a reputation second only to that of Upholder'.

The names of the personnel lost in Urge were recorded on official naval memorials after the War, according to their division, and include those at Portsmouth, Plymouth and Chatham. A full list also appears in the area of remembrance at the Royal Navy Submarine Museum in Gosport, Hampshire. An alphabetical list of names has been placed beneath the new National Submarine Memorial.

St.Paul's window, donated by Mrs. Tomkinson, 1944

Detail from St.Paul's window

Lieutenant-Commander Tomkinson and Urge's successes were shown in a picture in the HMS Dolphin Wardroom along with Lieutenant-Commander Wanklyn and Upholder's. Mrs.Tomkinson and Mrs.Wanklyn became close friends, just as their husbands had been, and kept in contact for many years.

In 1975, one of several new accommodation blocks for junior rates at HMS Dolphin was named after Lieutenant-Commander Tomkinson (the other four blocks were named after famous Second World War commanders Wanklyn

Detail of kneeler embroidered by Jackman family in memory of CPO Charley Jackman

Detail of Urge ship's badge on kneeler by Jackman family

Church candlesticks inscribed to the memory of ERA Eric Varley, donated by his parents

Urge brooch given to his family by PO Tel Peter Wiseman

VC, Miers VC, Linton VC and Cameron VC). At the opening, Admiral Miers, VC said that Lieutenant-Commander Tomkinson 'had a special flair for submarine warfare backed by self-confidence and good judgment…tenacity and concentration. Beloved by his crew, his record was phenomenal'.

25/2/48 -

My dear Mrs Tomkinson.

I feel I must explain myself first as we have not met, though I knew Tommo very well, and was beaten at golf by him with regularity. I am now Captain S/M V, i.e. Captain of Blockhouse. We have just taken over some new buildings at Hornet, and the blocks are being named after submariners who distinguished themselves in World War II, and of course URGE has a block named after her. I have obtained a short record of achievement of Urge

Letter from Captain Ben Bryant of HMS Dolphin about the naming of a building there after Urge, 1948

Captain L. H. OLIPHANT, DSC, Royal Navy
requests the pleasure of the company of

Mrs E. Tomkinson

in HMS DOLPHIN
at 1430 on WEDNESDAY, 19th MARCH, 1975
at the
OFFICIAL OPENING
of the
PHYSICAL AND RECREATIONAL TRAINING CENTRE
(Miers Block)
and the
NEW JUNIOR RATINGS' ACCOMMODATION
(Cameron, Linton, Tomkinson and Wanklyn Blocks)
by
Rear Admiral Sir ANTHONY MIERS, VC KBE CB DSO*
and the relatives of the late
Commander D. CAMERON, VC RN
Commander J. W. LINTON, VC DSO DSC RN
Lieutenant Commander E. P. TOMKINSON, DSO* RN
and
Lieutenant Commander M. D. WANKLYN, VC DSO** RN

RSVP The Commander's Assistant
HMS DOLPHIN
Fort Blockhouse
Gosport, PO12 2AD

Dress : No. 5 (Uniform)
Lounge Suit

your honour's

Invitation to the official opening of the Tomkinson Block and other buildings, HMS Dolphin, 1975

H.M.S. DOLPHIN

OFFICIAL OPENING

of the

PHYSICAL AND

RECREATIONAL TRAINING CENTRE

(MIERS BLOCK)

and the

NEW JUNIOR RATINGS' ACCOMMODATION

(CAMERON, LINTON, TOMKINSON AND
WANKLYN BLOCKS)

on

WEDNESDAY, 19th MARCH, 1975

at 1430

Programme for the opening of the Tomkinson Block and other buildings named after World War II COs, HMS Dolphin, 1975

PROGRAMME

Incidental music whilst guests assemble

Guests are requested to be seated by 1428

At 1430 Rear Admiral Sir Anthony Miers, VC KBE CB DSO* arrives, escorted by Captain L. H. Oliphant, DSC Royal Navy, Captain, HMS Dolphin.

National Anthem

Captain Oliphant makes a speech of welcome

Rear Admiral Miers replies on behalf of the guests

Presentation of keys to the relatives of the distinguished submariners after whom the Blocks are to be named

Presentation of scissors to Rear Admiral Miers

Fanfare by Herald Trumpeters

Rear Admiral Miers cuts the tape and declares MIERS Block open.

Rear Admiral Miers escorted on tour of MIERS Block

Relatives of distinguished submariners, together with visiting dignatories and members of the ships company, escorted to the appropriate blocks for opening ceremonies

Fanfare by Herald Trumpeters

Relatives simultaneously unlock Main Entrance of respective accommodation blocks, declare them open and tour the accommodation, returning to MIERS block for Afternoon Tea

NOTE.—In the event of inclement weather, the relatives and a small group of visiting dignatories will perform the accommodation block opening ceremonies. The remaining guests and ships company will watch the TOMKINSON Block opening ceremony, and then tour all the buildings, returning to MIERS Block for Afternoon Tea

8

THE DISCOVERY OF HMS URGE'S WRECK

In 2017 an international maritime project called Project Spur was formed to plan and organise a search for Urge's wreck. Each of the joint leaders of the project had a special interest in the submarine. Professor Timmy Gambin of the Department of Classics and Archeology at the University of Malta is a leading international authority on maritime archeology. Francis Dickinson is a grandson of Lieutenant-Commander Tomkinson with particular knowledge of Urge's history, and was the lead sponsor for the project. Platon Alexiades is a Canadian naval research expert with detailed knowledge of relevant World War II records, and also sponsored the project. Project Spur was formed under the auspices of the University of Malta's Research, Innovation and Development Trust. In 2012 Professor Gambin had discovered the wreck of another British submarine HMS Olympus, which succumbed to a German mine a few days after Urge had disappeared.

Urge's deck gun and conning tower emerge in the first images of the wreck, 2019

Divers led by Timmy Gambin visit the wreck, 2021

In 2019 a search at sea off Malta led by Professor Gambin in co-ordination with Maltese authorities located Urge's wreck around two miles off Fort St.Elmo, Malta. A German mine laid in April, 1942 was indeed found to have been the cause of the loss. The successful search involved the project's joint leaders, all of whom were in search vessels off the coast at the time of the discovery, and an international team of maritime archeologists drawn from staff and students based at the University of Malta as well as in the United States. A number of different vessels and remote operating vehicles were used to evaluate the seabed where German and Italian minefields had been laid in Urge's path. In 2021, following delays caused by the Coronavirus pandemic, Professor Gambin was able to lead a specialist team of divers to examine the wreck, obtaining further detailed imagery at a depth of well over 300 feet and providing final certainty on the identification. The UK Ministry of Defence has recognised the wreck as the last resting place of those lost aboard Urge.

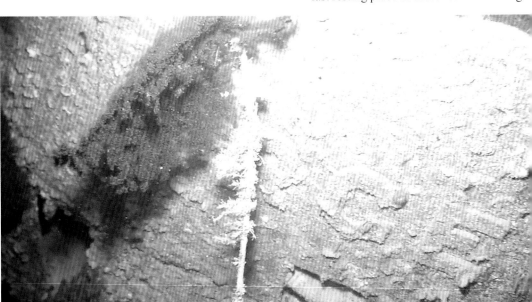
Urge's conning tower, with letters spelling out the name in capitals, 2021

Divers examine the conning tower, 2021; note the remains of 'jumping wires' designed to help the submarine clear obstacles

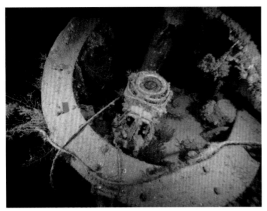

Conning tower with compass binnacle   *12 pounder gun*

In due course further analysis is expected to enhance our understanding of the events which occurred on 27th April, 1942 and Urge's wreck site. The Virtual Museum of Underwater Malta promotes public awareness and understanding of the value and importance of underwater cultural heritage, including war graves, and forms part of Malta's continuing custodianship of Urge's last resting place.

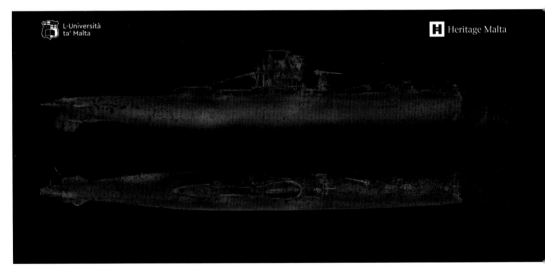

University of Malta/Heritage Malta diagram of Urge's wreck

9

PEOPLE WHO LEFT HMS URGE BEFORE THE LOSS

There were no survivors when Urge sank on 27th April, 1942. However, a number of people who served on the submarine went on to other roles before the loss and survived the War. The remnants of the 10th Flotilla reached Alexandria, but then had to evacuate again to Palestine, eventually returning to re-establish in Malta in August, 1942.

Lieutenant Sam Marriott had been the initial first lieutenant before Lieutenant Malcolm Poole, leaving Urge to take up his own successful commands in home waters and the Far East (retiring as Captain Marriott, DSO, DSC). His younger son, Major General Patrick Marriott, CB, CBE, recalls his father reflecting how much he had learned from Lieutenant-Commander Tomkinson and Urge, and that without that early mentoring he would never have made it through the War -"Tommo' was such a wonderful example to him. He was the paladin that I think my father most missed after the War.'

Captain Sam Marriott   *Rear Admiral Godfrey Place*   *Lt Col Robert Wilson*

Lieutenant Ian McGeoch, who had been on board Urge for passage to Malta from the UK, later became an effective submarine commander, as well as escaping from enemy captivity after being captured when his submarine was destroyed. He became Vice Admiral Sir Ian McGeoch KCB, DSO, DSC and held senior defence roles.

Lieutenant Godfrey Place served on Urge during the December, 1941 patrol when the Vittorio Veneto was torpedoed, leaving after that patrol as he had been standing in for a permanent crew member who returned after illness. Later in the War, Place was awarded the VC for his famous midget submarine attack on the German battleship Tirpitz, so he had two successful battleship attacks to his credit. He became Rear Admiral Place, VC, CB, DSC, and remembered Lieutenant-Commander Tomkinson as 'a very capable submarine captain and a most delightful man.'.

In 1986 CPO Wheeler and Bill Haines, as veterans who had formerly served on Urge, signed an Armed Forces Postal Service first day cover depicting Urge's Bande Nere sinking. Another similar first day cover was signed by the Flag Officer Submarines at the time. CPO Wheeler was subsequently mentioned in despatches for submarine service in the Far East.

A number of other sailors went on to roles in other submarines including Petty Officers such as Alfred Curtis, DSM* and Benjamin Hughes DSM. Sadly, some were themselves later lost in action. One of these, Able Seaman David Miller, was awarded the DSM for his service on Urge, and then transferred to become 2nd Coxswain in Upholder, where he was awarded a Bar to the DSM after being lost. PO Hughes wrote of his sadness at receiving his decoration at Buckingham Palace without his former shipmates.

Of the SBS commandos, Captain Wilson and Marine Hughes who blew up the first of Urge's enemy trains survived the War. 'Tug' Wilson was captured in later missions, went on to fight in the Korean War, and became a Lieutenant-Colonel with a DSO and Bar. Lieutenant TGA Walker and Sergeant HHV Penn were the SBS commandos who blew up Urge's second enemy train.

10

CONNECTIONS WITH MALTA AND OTHER NATIONS

View from the site of the HMS Urge Memorial, Fort St Elmo

As with all the 10th Flotilla submariners, Urge's crew formed close bonds with the people of Malta. One of them, Telegraphist Henry Twist, married a Maltese bride, Salvina Borg, in 1941. Although most of the 10th Flotilla submarines were British, some were manned by crews from other countries. Urge had a particular friendship with the Polish submarine ORP Sokol (commanded by Lieutenant Borys Karnicki, formerly HMS Urchin), and the submariners were visited by General Sikorski of Poland. Sokol closely resembled Urge, and was one of a number of Allied boats crewed from occupied European countries including Norway, Holland, France and Greece. The SIS agent at the centre of Urge's missions in Sicily in October, 1941 and February, 1942 was the French national Alfred Rossi. The SIS agent which Urge landed in Tunisia in February, 1942 was Philippe Saillard, a Frenchman who operated as a successful agent for the Allies and went on to other missions in France later in the War.

The search for and work relating to Urge's wreck involved people from Malta, the UK, Canada, the United States, Spain, Italy and Poland among other countries.

In 2022 a memorial to all those lost in Urge is being officially dedicated in Malta. It is situated at Fort St.Elmo, and the names of those remembered will face to sea where their last resting place lies. The work has involved the families of those lost in Urge, Heritage Malta, the University of Malta, and architects, designers, stone masons, planning authorities and builders. Urge is also remembered in St.Paul's Pro-Cathedral, Valletta, Malta.

11

AFFILIATION WITH THE TOWN OF BRIDGEND

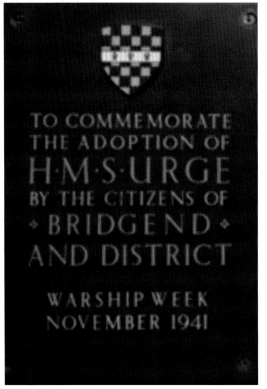

Plaque commemorating Bridgend's affiliation with Urge

British towns and cities created affiliations by "adopting" RN ships and submarines during World War II, providing finance and forming bonds with the fighting forces. As part of Warship Week in November, 1941, the town of Bridgend adopted Urge, raising significant funds towards the cost of the submarine. In his last letter home Lieutenant-Commander Tomkinson mentioned he had just received a letter from the Mayor of Bridgend.

The town mourned Urge's loss, and has had a particular interest in remembrance of those lost ever since. Bridgend Town Council has the original War Office Ship's Badge for Urge and has valuable continuing links with crew family members. Local work on the submarine's history includes a mural and studies about the achievements of Urge.

Sub-Lieutenant Brian Lloyd, who was killed in a special mission in October, 1941, was from Bridgend. Lieutenant-Commander Tomkinson considered Sub-Lieutenant Lloyd to have shown great promise and that he would have been an excellent submarine officer. Sub-Lieutenant Lloyd is buried at Catania military cemetery in Sicily.

Mural of Urge in Bridgend; the submarine appears to dive at high water

Brian made his last journey on this Submarine, end of Sept or first two days of Oct. 1941.

NATIONAL SAVINGS MOVEMENT

BRIDGEND AND DISTRICT WARSHIP WEEK

Souvenir Programme

Adoption of H.M.S. "Urge"

Submarine of abt. 750 tons

Ceremony for the Exchange of Plaques

AT THE

Embassy Cinema, Bridgend

ON

Sunday, 28th February, 1943

AT 2.30 P.M.

ADMIRALTY REPRESENTATIVE : THE RT. HON. GEORGE H. HALL, M.P.,
Financial Secretary to the Admiralty

CHAIRMAN : TED WILLIAMS, ESQ., M.P.

Programme from Bridgend's adoption ceremony for Urge, 1943

12

HMS URGE: FACTS AND FIGURES

Built by Vickers-Armstrongs Limited, Barrow-in-Furness

Pennant number: P40/N17 (Second group U class)

Battle honours: Mediterranean 1941-2; Malta Convoys

Ship's badge: Two interlocking spurs on a blue background (motto: "Spur on")

Ordered: 4 Sepember, 1939. Laid down: 30 October, 1939. Launched: 19 August, 1940. Commissioned/ completed: 12 December, 1940. Lost: 27 April, 1942.

Length: 196 ft. Maximum beam: 16 ft. Safe diving depth: 250 ft

Surface displacement: 646 tons

Complement: 4 Officers, 28 ratings. In addition Urge was carrying 11 naval passengers and one civilian passenger at the time of loss.

Armament: 8 x 21 inch torpedoes (maximum salvo of 4); 1 x 12 pounder deck gun; 2/3 x Lewis machine guns

6 Main ballast tanks to enable diving and surfacing, 2 sets of hydraulically operated hydroplanes to control depth.

Machinery: Twin propellers, generated by 615 bhp Paxman diesel engine when on the surface, main battery when dived.

Speed: Maximum surface speed 11.75 knots, dived speed 8 knots (in practice slower speeds were used to conserve power, typically around 9/10 knots when surfaced and much slower speeds when submerged)

Pressure hull of circular cross section; submarine divided into 6 compartments by bulkheads. Above pressure hull was conning tower with bridge; aft but mainly forward of the conning tower was the casing, a lighter, free draining metal platform for crew members to stand on.

3 points of access: fore hatch (used for loading torpedoes), conning tower hatches or engine room hatch

2 periscopes, used from control room; the search periscope was more powerful but larger and more likely to be sighted; the attack periscope was thinner but low magnification lens only.

The ASDIC set (named after the Anti-Submarine and Detection Investigation Committee, later known as SONAR or Sound Navigation and Ranging) and hydrophones enabled listening and detection of the enemy. Wireless transmissions were through an aerial when surfaced, and raising the W/T mast when dived.

Patrol duration: Up to 2 weeks.

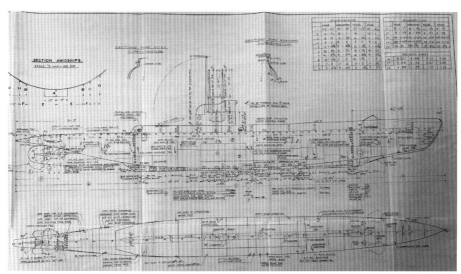

Constructor's drawings of U class submarines including Urge

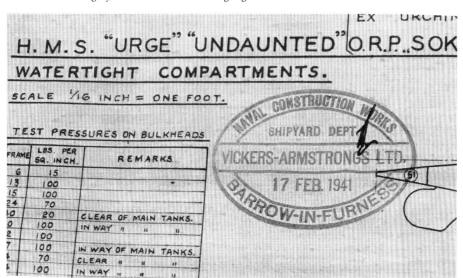

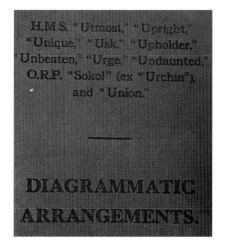

HMS URGE: PATROL SUMMARY AND CHRONOLOGY

Urge undertook 20 war patrols. Lieutenant-Commander Tomkinson was in command for all except two patrols.

Working up exercises were as part of 3rd Submarine Flotilla (HMS Forth), Holy Loch area, December, 1940.

Urge was subsequently attached to 9th Submarine Flotilla (Dundee). Exercises with RN anti-submarine forces took place at Scapa Flow during January, 1941.

NORTH SEA WAR PATROLS:

Patrol 1 (8-15 Feb, 1941): Norway (search for German warships including cruiser Hipper).
Patrol 2 (25 Feb-12 Mar, 1941): Norway (Sub Lt Catlow landed in the UK, injured by scalding on pipe)

Passage to Gibraltar from Portsmouth (14-23 April, 1941) : Sank the enemy tanker Franco Martelli (10,800 tons) in Bay of Biscay. Recommendations for awards made.

Passage to Malta after engine work in Gibraltar (departed 28 April, arrived Marsamxett Harbour, Malta 6 May, 1941).

MEDITERRANEAN WAR PATROLS:

Urge undertook 18 patrols as part of the 10th Submarine Flotilla ('The Fighting Tenth'), HMS Talbot. During this period enemy air attacks became consistently heavier and in 1942 in particular Urge often came back to find either the 10th Flotilla's Manoel Island base, other submarines or their own accommodation (or all three) had been or even were being bombed.

Patrol 1 (14 - 22 May, 1941): Tunisia. Several attacks on enemy ships; depth charges and heavy explosions experienced; dive to 278 ft to avoid enemy attack exceeds design specifications. Recommendations for awards made.

Patrol 2 (1 - 12 June, 1941): Lampedusa Island/Tunisia. Unsuccessful attack on zigzagging enemy convoy.

Patrol 3 (23 June - 4 July, 1941): Straits of Messina, in company two other submarines. Later, Urge landed SBS commandos (Captain Wilson/Marine Hughes) for first successful demolition mission of enemy munitions train on 27 June; the explosion of the train was watched from the submarine which then observed enemy repairs for several nights. Further attacks on convoys and enemy ships including heavy depth charging.

Patrol 4 (18 July - 29 July, 1941): North coast of Sicily. Urge was second submarine to pioneer new route through dangerous enemy minefield QBB 65. Unsuccessful attack on small freighter. SBS aboard. Lieutenant Tomkinson experienced severe back pain and was admitted to hospital for one patrol on return.

Patrol 5 (7 August - 15 August, 1941): Straits of Messina. Lieutenant CP Norman temporarily in command. Port engine failure necessitated early return to base.

Patrol 6 (18 August - 20 August, 1941): Tunisia. Lieutenant Tomkinson resumed command. Urge attempted an attack on enemy convoy but was hunted by aircraft and escorting destroyers before attack can be made.

Patrol 7 (25 August - 1 September, 1941): Marittimo – Naples – Messina – Palermo. Urge attacks convoy but one torpedo jams in its tube forcing the boat to surface in sight of the enemy; torpedo shaken clear; attack was successful hitting MV Aquitania. Further attack made on another convoy near Capri. 'High standard of skill, courage and discipline throughout the submarine' is praised, as is Lieutenant Tomkinson's 'outstanding courage and judgment'. Recommendations for awards made.

Patrol 8 (22 September - 5 October, 1941): Palermo. Attack on enemy merchant vessel, and then another on German U boat (U331) both fail due to faults with torpedo gyros, causing torpedoes to circle and explode violently under Urge; on the second occasion Urge surfaced to attempt gun action against U331 but the U boat dived having seen the track of the one torpedo which ran correctly. Urge was hunted by enemy ships around time of special mission to land SIS agent. Sub-Lieutenant Brian Lloyd killed in folbot operation to recover agent (Alfred Rossi) on 2nd October. Lieutenant-Commander Tomkinson and crew extricated Urge from enemy trap. Leading Signalman Eric Law was commended for watchfulness in sighting enemy vessel sent to ambush Urge.

Patrol 9 (14 - 16 October, 1941): East coast of Sicily. Sailed with 2 other submarines to intercept reported enemy forces but none sighted.

Patrol 10 (18 - 28 October, 1941): Tunisia. Attacked enemy merchant ship, believed hit but no explosion. Subsequently encountered larger enemy merchant ship Marigola (6,000 tons) aground on a shoal, which Urge torpedoed and sank in shallow water (the RAF and another submarine also attacked this vessel). Heavy weather damage led to fuel leak (10 tons lost in 36 hours). Defects to starboard generator. CERA Charles Toms' zeal and professional ability in charge of engines commended.

Patrol 11 (8 - 21 November, 1941): Italy to Benghazi convoy route. Searched for remnants of enemy forces destroyed by Force K. Unsuccessful attack on convoy due to error in implementing CO's orders on torpedo intervals, and long range. Very rough and squally weather; Captain (S10) describes position-keeping of Urge as 'commendable'.

Patrol 12 (10 - 20 December, 1941): Straits of Messina. Concentrated enemy E boat, aircraft and shore activity. Sighted enemy battleships Vittorio Veneto and Littorio with heavy escort. Fired full salvo of 4 torpedoes at 3,000 yards. Littorio sighted and evaded torpedoes, Vittorio Veneto hit on starboard side aft of rear turret and seriously damaged (out of action for three critical months, 40 enemy personnel killed). 40 depth charge counter attack/intense anti-submarine activity. Air raid in progress on return to Malta. Captain S10 - 'The whole conduct of the patrol reflects great credit on Lieutenant-Commander Tomkinson and his command.' Praise endorsed and echoed by Admiral AB Cunningham, RN C-in-C Med. Recommendations for awards to follow.

29 December, 1941: Urge and Upholder (both with temporary COs in command) conducted exercises with HMS Beryl (armed trawler) off Valletta. German Messerschmitt Bf 109 fighters attack both submarines, injuring temporary CO on Upholder. Urge dives in time to avoid serious damage from cannon and machine gun fire.

Patrol 13 (30 December, 1941- 11 January, 1942): Lampion Island - Tunisia. Lieutenant JD Martin temporarily in command for one patrol (uneventful).

Patrol 14 (22 January - 3 February, 1942): Tripoli – Malta – Sicily. Lieutenant-Commander Tomkinson resumed command. Italian U boat sighted but dived before intended attack on it could be made. Urge was recalled to Malta briefly on 26 January. Targets sighted but at very long range; one convoy attack 29 depth charge counter attack.

Patrol 15 (12 - 26 February, 1942): Tunisia - Sicily. SBS aboard for special operations. Captain Wilson landed SIS agent Philippe Saillard from Urge in Tunisia; Wilson was then found and recovered with difficulty by Urge in rough seas (his folbot, smashed by the waves and a capsize, had to be abandoned). Heavy weather prevented a further planned mission in this area, which was in fact heavily mined by the enemy; at least three other U class submarines were lost in the area, including one on a similar mission to Urge's on this patrol. In Sicily, SBS were to land parcel for SIS agent. However, Lieutenant-Commander Tomkinson was highly suspicious after the incident in Mediterranean Patrol 8 with the same agent, and approached the coast with great caution. This concern was justified, as Rossi had been captured and was operating his radio under Italian control. Attempted enemy trap evaded by Urge. Admiral Harwood (the new RN C-in-C Med) stated that Lieutenant-Commander Tomkinson's 'sound judgment' and 'the efficiency of Urge's lookout' saved the submarine from an ambush.

26 February - 9 March, 1942: Urge underwent repairs (refit) in Malta, including replacing port generator. Intensive work period for Lieutenant-Commander Tomkinson and crew, in particular ERAs and stokers.

Patrol 16 (9 - 14 March, 1942): North of Sicily. Sailed direct from Malta dockyard. Search for enemy shipping; patrol curtailed due to main engine defects (new port generator defective).

Further engine work (15 - 22 March, 1942): main generators changed again.

Patrol 17: (23 March - 6 April, 1942): South of Naples, north of Sicily. SBS (Lieutenant Walker/Sergeant Penn) landed by Urge for successful further train demolition special mission, train blown up and rolled down embankment. Meanwhile, Urge sighted enemy merchant ship; torpedo attack missed as was forced early at long range in squalls/darkness due to train explosion; Urge chased enemy ship on the surface, achieving hits with her deck gun and machine gun fire. Near misses of return fire soaked those on the bridge and Lieutenant-Commander Tomkinson decided the action was too dangerous to continue and ordered Urge to dive. On 1 April he sighted an enemy naval force led by the 6 inch gun cruiser Giovanni Delle Bande Nere, which had just taken part in the Second Battle of Sirte causing RN casualties, and attacked at a range of 5,000 yards. Bande Nere was hit by 2 torpedoes and sank in 8 minutes, with the loss of more than half her crew. Admiral Harwood: 'This very successful patrol reflects great credit on all concerned.'. Senior officers called this a 'typical Tomkinson patrol' 'conducted with Lieutenant-Commander Tomkinson's usual precision and determination.' Recommendations for awards made.

7 - 10 April: Urge's crew at rest camp while spare crew manned and overhauled the submarine.

Patrol 18 (11 - 22 April, 1942): Tunisia. Attack on convoy failed when enemy aircraft sighted torpedoes and convoy took avoiding action. Bad visibility and gales.

After a total of 20 war patrols, passage from Malta to Alexandria: Lieutenant-Commander Tomkinson was by now the senior CO of the 10th Flotilla. Urge sailed 27 April, 1942 at 4.45am and proceeded by a route from St.Elmo Lighthouse to Alexandria (P31 had sailed on the same route 24 hours previously). After 6th May, 1942 Urge was overdue, and in due course her loss had to be accepted.

THOSE LOST IN HM SUBMARINE URGE ON 27 APRIL, 1942, TOGETHER WITH RANKS AND AWARDS

LIEUTENANT-COMMANDER EP TOMKINSON DSO AND BAR
(AWARDED TWO YEARS' SENIORITY FOR MERITORIOUS WAR SERVICE, MID, FURTHER
AWARDS PENDING AT DATE OF LOSS)
LIEUTENANT JMS POOLE DSC AND BAR
LIEUTENANT JSD RANSOME DSC
LIEUTENANT DB ALLEN DSC (MID)
CHIEF PETTY OFFICER CJ JACKMAN DSM AND BAR (MID TWICE, LSGC MEDAL)
PETTY OFFICER HRJ WATTS DSM (MID)
LEADING SEAMAN LF GROVES DSM
LEADING SEAMAN J NORRIS DSM
LEADING SEAMAN HGA OSBORN DSM
ABLE SEAMAN LG BAXTER
ABLE SEAMAN R DAVISON
ABLE SEAMAN F DAY
ABLE SEAMAN RH GOSS (MID)
ABLE SEAMAN J O'NEILL (MID)
ABLE SEAMAN JL PARKINSON
ABLE SEAMAN JK ROWLEY DSM
ABLE SEAMAN R WILDMAN
PETTY OFFICER TELEGRAPHIST PD WISEMAN (MID)
LEADING TELEGRAPHIST HG ASHFORD
LEADING TELEGRAPHIST J MAIDMENT
TELEGRAPHIST HE TWIST DSM
LEADING SIGNALMAN EC LAW (MID)
CHIEF ENGINE ROOM ARTIFICER CH TOMS DSM (LSGC MEDAL)
ENGINE ROOM ARTIFICER R HELLYER DSM
ENGINE ROOM ARTIFICER E VARLEY (MID)
STOKER PETTY OFFICER WG ASHFORD DSM
LEADING STOKER JW LAMB
LEADING STOKER JE WOOLRICH

STOKER C BROWN
STOKER AE BRYANT (MID)
STOKER JCD MCMILLAN (MID)
STOKER M STANGER

PASSENGERS, FORMER CREW:

LEADING TELEGRAPHIST RWG ROGERS DSM
LEADING SIGNALMAN RW LEEKE
ENGINE ROOM ARTIFICER SG HARMAN

PASSENGERS:

PETTY OFFICER HJ BOTTING
LEADING SEAMAN SW CHAMBERLAIN
LEADING SEAMAN FH MORRIS
ABLE SEAMAN F MCDIARMID
ENGINE ROOM ARTIFICER RF RUTTER
ENGINE ROOM ARTIFICER WP WHITE
LEADING STOKER SC WILKES
STOKER RH ATTEWELL
MR. B GRAY

LOST ON A SPECIAL MISSION FROM HM SUBMARINE URGE
ON 2 OCTOBER, 1941

SUB-LIEUTENANT BNT LLOYD

A NOTE ON SOURCES

The dates and technical details of patrols are derived from patrol reports held at the National Archives (NA). The NA also hold casualty files and some citations for awards. Almost all Lieutenant-Commander Tomkinson's 60 letters home from Malta survive, along with Mrs.Tomkinson's correspondence with HMS Urge crew family members in 1942 onwards. Letters from and interviews with veterans have supplemented books and speeches by senior submariners and historians. Naval records from both sides have also become available through original material and summaries by researchers.

Selected further reading featuring HMS Urge/Lieutenant-Commander Tomkinson:

An Affair of Chances, Vice-Admiral Sir Ian McGeoch, KCB, DSO, DSC; IWM 1991
British and Allied Submarine Operations in World War II, Vice-Admiral Sir Arthur Hezlet, KBE, CB, DSO*, DSC; RNSM, 2001
British Submarines at War, Alastair Mars, DSO DSC*; William Kimber, 1971
Fighting Under the Sea, Captain Donald Macintrye, DSO**, DSC; Evans Brothers, 1965
Half-Time, Commander Anthony Kimmins, OBE; Heinemann, 1947
Periscope Patrol, John Frayn Turner; Harrap, 1957
Periscope View, Rear-Admiral GWG Simpson, CB, CBE; Macmillan, 1972
The Battle for the Mediterranean, Captain Donald Macintyre, DSO**, DSC; Batsford, 1964
The Fighting Tenth, John Wingate DSC; Leo Cooper, 1991
The Sword of Damocles, Vice-Admiral Sir Hugh Mackenzie, KCB, DSO*, DSC; RNSM, 1995
General accounts of experiences in WW2 submarines:
Submariner, Charles Anscomb, William Kimber, 1957
Submarine Command, Rear-Admiral Ben Bryant, CB, DSO**, DSC, William Kimber (originally published as One Band Band, 1958)
Unbroken, the Story of a Submarine, Alastair Mars, DSO, DSC* (originally published by Frederick Muller in 1953)
Fiction mentioning HMS Urge includes Submariner, Alexander Fullerton, Sphere, 2008 (see also A Share of Honour by the same author

Primary sources (UK National Archives):
HMS Urge Patrol Reports
HMS Urge Ship's Log
HMS Urge Casualty Files
HMS Urge Awards Citations
Primary sources (Axis records):
German Naval Records, National Archives, College Park, Maryland, USA
Italian Naval Records, Ufficio Storico Della Marina Militare, Rome

ILLUSTRATIONS

Every effort has been made to attribute photographic credits correctly. Any clarifications would be welcomed and appear in future editions.

Front page: RNSM (part of the NMRN), inside front cover: F.Dickinson (FD), Opposite title page: FD, page 8 FD, 11 S.McGeoch, 12 FD, 14 FD, 15 (all) FD, 16 (top) FD, 17 FD, 18-19 RNSM, 20 RNSM, 21 RNSM, 22 RNSM, 23 RNSM, 24 FD, 25 (top left) Bundesarchiv, 25 (top right and lower) RNSM, 26 FD, 27 (all) FD, 28 (all) FD, 29 FD, (RNSM), 30 (left) Jackman family/ RNSM, 30 (middle) P.Steed, 30 (right) V.Doty, 31 (top left) FD, 31 (top middle) A.Law/A.Robinson, 31 (top right) FD, 31 (lower left) RNSM, 31 (lower right), S./A.Foster, 32 (top left) J.Wood, 32 (top middle) A.Martin, 32 (top right) Twist family/RNSM, 32 (lower left) R.Bowes, 32 (lower middle) A.Tillson, 32 (lower right) RNSM, 33 FD, 34 Imperial War Museum (IWM), 35 (top left) RNSM, 35 (top middle) FD, 35 (top right) A.John, 35 (lower left and right) RNSM, 36 (top) Ufficio Storico della Marina Militare (USMM), 36 (lower left and right) FD, 37 (top) M.Cigogna collection, 37 (lower) USMM, 38 and 39 (both) USMM, 40 (top three) USMM, 40 (lower) FD, 41 (top) C.Lloyd, 41 (lower) RNSM, 42 (top) RNSM, 42 (lower) FD, 43 (top) IWM, 43 (lower left) Jackman family/RNSM, 43 (lower right) J.Wood, 44 RNSM, 45 (lower) H.Broome, 46 (top left and lower left and right) Bundesarchiv, 46 (top right) RNSM, 47 FD, 48 Jackman family/RNSM, 49 (right) J.Wilkes/Z.Wilkes, 50 FD, 51 FD, 52 (top) RNSM, 52 (middle) A.Martin, 52 (lower) FD, 53 (all) FD, 54 (top left) E.Varley, 54 (top right, lower left and right) FD, 55 and 56 FD, 57, 58 (both), 59, 60 (all) The University of Malta/Heritage Malta (UoM/HM), 61 (left) P.Marriott, 61 (middle and right) RNSM, 63-64 (all) FD, 65 C.Lloyd, 67 (all) FD, 74 FD, inside back cover RNSM, back cover (top) RNSM, back cover (lower) FD.

Back cover image: HMS Urge at HMS Talbot, the base of the 10th Submarine Flotilla, Manoel Island, Malta Lt-Cdr EP Tomkinson, DSO*, RN, CO of HMS Urge.

Officers and men from the 10th Submarine Flotilla, together with SBS commandos, HMS *Talbot*, Manoel Island. Many of those sitting behind Lt-Cdr Tomkinson in the 3rd row back were in *Urge's* ship's company. Note rubble from bomb damage in the foreground